The Science of Self Talk:
How to Increase Your Emotional Intelligence and Stop Getting in Your Own Way

Positive Psychology Coaching Series

Copyright © 2018 by Ian Tuhovsky

Author's blog: www.mindfulnessforsuccess.com
Author's Amazon profile: amazon.com/author/iantuhovsky
Instagram profile: https://instagram.com/mindfulnessforsuccess

All rights reserved. No part of this publication may be reproduced, stored in a retrieval system, or transmitted, in any form or by any means, electronic, mechanical, photocopying, recording or otherwise without the prior written permission of the author and the publishers.

The scanning, uploading, and distribution of this book via the Internet, or via any other means, without the permission of the author is illegal and punishable by law.

Please purchase only authorized electronic editions, and do not participate in or encourage electronic piracy of copyrighted materials.

Important

The book is not intended to provide medical advice or to take the place of medical advice and treatment from your personal physician. Readers are advised to consult their own doctors or other qualified health professionals regarding the treatment of medical conditions. The author shall not be held liable or responsible for any misunderstanding or misuse of the information contained in this book. The information is not indeed to diagnose, treat or cure any disease.

It's important to remember that the author of this book is not a doctor/therapist/medical professional. Only opinions based upon his own personal experiences or research are cited. The author does not offer medical advice or prescribe any treatments. For any health or medical issues – you should be talking to your doctor first.

Please be aware that every e-book and "short read" I publish is truly written by me, with thoroughly researched content 100% of the time. Unfortunately, there's a huge number of low quality, cheaply outsourced spam titles on Kindle non-fiction market these days, created by various Internet marketing companies. **I don't tolerate these books. I want to provide you with high quality, so** <u>if you think that one of my books/short reads can be improved in some way, please contact me at:</u>

contact@mindfulnessforsuccess.com

<u>I will be very happy to hear from you, because you are who I write my books for!</u>

Introduction	5
Chapter 1 – What Is Self-Talk?	6
Exercise I	8
Chapter 2 – Constructive Self-Talk, Dysfunctional Self-Talk	9
Exercise II	10
Chapter 3 – Impact of Negative Self-Talk	12
Learned Helplessness	16
Exercise III	18
Chapter 4 – Positive Self-Talk	20
Challenge or Threat?	21
Self-Leadership	22
Self-Deception and False Positivity	23
Examples of Self-Talk	25
Exercise IV	27
Chapter 5 – Pareto: The 80/20 Rule	29
Chapter 6 – Creating the Right Circumstances for Motivation	33
Chapter 7 – The Self	37
Chapter 8 – Loving Yourself	40
Emotional Intelligence	41
Present and Future Selves	41
Chapter 9 – Getting to Know Yourself	44
Swimming in the OCEAN	44
Exercise V	49
Chapter 10 – Who's Talking?	51
Exercise VI	52
Chapter 11 – What's in a Pronoun?	54
Exercise VII	55
Chapter 12 – Turning Down the Volume	57
Addendum: Specific Applications	59
Mistakes	59
Health and Exercise	60
Wealth and Career	61
Relationships	63
My Free Gift to You – Get One of My Audiobooks For Free!	65
Recommended Reading for You	68
Take control of your future with life-changing learning skills.	76
About The Author	86

Introduction

Have you ever paid attention to your inner speech? You know, that running conversation that seems to go on interminably in your head. The one that's in the background, thinking your thoughts, or rather "speaking" them to you in an internal, or is it infernal, commentary?

Or did you just kind of ignore it, never really thinking much about it? But I bet you're thinking about it, now that I've mentioned it. And even if you're thinking, "I have absolutely no idea what you're talking about," stop and listen to your thoughts for a second. Chances are, you're thinking in a *voice* with *speech*. *That's* what I'm talking about.

What causes us to talk to ourselves silently or out loud? How does self-talk affect our emotions and actions? "How can we become more aware of what we're saying to ourselves?

These are interesting questions and we'll get to them, but, by far, the most useful question we can ask is: Can we talk to ourselves differently? Can we flip the script and rewrite the way we communicate with ourselves?

The answer is, yes, we can. And that's what this book is about.

Chapter 1 – What Is Self-Talk?

Let's start with a more precise definition. Self-talk, aka *intra*personal communication, is your internal use of speech and language. It appears in the form of thoughts that you can "hear" with the auditory part of your brain.

It can also include speaking to yourself out loud. Which is totally normal, I promise. Well, unless you're experiencing hallucinations and hearing voices, in which case it could be a serious problem requiring the attention of a mental health professional. But maybe you don't want to do it when others are around. Definitely avoid mumbling to yourself as you walk down the street or browse the aisles in the supermarket.

(See? We're only getting started and already you have actionable advice for how *not* to self-talk. You're welcome.)

If you still don't get what I'm talking about, notice what happens as you're reading these words. Read them silently, but pay attention to your thoughts. Do you "hear" the words in your head as you read them? That's also self-talk. If you're like most people, you use the same inner voice to speak to yourself in a variety of situations virtually all the time.

Much of the time, we don't really notice our self-talk, so it's this kind of half-conscious chatter going on at the edges of our awareness like smatterings of conversations in nearby cubicles at work. But we all listen in pretty regularly, as well. The conversation usually comments on ourselves, other people, and situations, which could be whatever is currently happening, or what did happen, or what we imagine is going to happen.

It's like turning on the director's commentary on a movie. There's the actual movie, which is our experience, and then there's whatever the director is saying *about* what's on the screen, which is our self-talk. Or you can think of it like a sports announcer commenting on the game as it's happening.

If you listen carefully, you'll notice that this inner conversation reflects thoughts and emotions. Self-talk isn't random. It exhibits patterns that repeat themselves. And everyone has their own characteristic self-talk that is uniquely theirs.

Some people's self-talk is mostly about the future, while others' is an internal dialogue about the past. Some self-talk tends to be positive and upbeat, while other self-talk is harsh and critical. Or it can be defeatist, gloomy, and negative. Sometimes, self-talk is focused more on people; sometimes, it's fixated more on things. Sometimes, it's mainly about others, and, sometimes, mainly about oneself.

One of the points we'll hammer home again and again is that it's important to listen to your self-talk and identify the patterns. If you do that, you'll learn a lot of useful things about yourself. And you'll figure out areas where you have a certain style of self-talk that's having a negative impact on your life. Once you know that, you can do something about it by talking to yourself differently.

That's important because negative self-talk is linked to negative emotional states such as anxiety, depression, insecurity, rumination, learned helplessness, and so on. In other words, a sense that life is too overwhelming, that you can't do much to improve your condition, and even if there were something you could do, you'd probably fail. Obviously, that's not a good place to be.

Positive self-talk, on the other hand, is linked with *less* negative emotion and more happiness, confidence, optimism, success in life, and a sense of agency and authorship of your own existence.

Okay, but how does that work? I'm going to argue that self-talk creates a feedback loop. What you put into it determines what comes out, and your reaction to that determines what you put into it the next time around. If you break a negative feedback loop by giving it a positive input instead, it will spin into a positive feedback loop. That creates a kind of snowball effect, which takes on a life of its own. Make a small, incremental change today, and it will gather momentum the next day, and the day after that, and the day after that... until you're surprised at what you've accomplished.

Exercise I

Spend some time with yourself, noticing your internal speech. It's best to do this while you're not very engaged with something. So put down the ebook, pocket your devices, and go for a walk in the park. Go sit on the porch or balcony. Just be by yourself for a time and listen to your inner dialogue. Don't try to change it; just relax and listen for now.

Repeat this exercise a few times, and you'll soon start to recognize characteristic patterns. Once you get used to that, then try to tune in when you're otherwise engaged with something.

Pay attention to what your inner speech is saying to you as you work, as you hang out with friends, as you wash the dishes, as you do anything. You'll get an idea of what your self-talk patterns are in various situations.

This isn't just a one-time exercise, it's a useful habit to train in yourself. At first, you have to make a conscious effort at it, but, with time, you'll just notice your self-talk automatically.

Chapter 2 – Constructive Self-Talk, Dysfunctional Self-Talk

Consider the sports commentary analogy from earlier. A sports announcer makes judgments of a player's performance as they're playing the game. Maybe he criticizes the player or maybe he praises a good performance.

Likewise, through self-talk your ego makes a lot of judgments about *you* and *your* performance as you do the things you do. Those judgments can be positive or negative. But positive and negative doesn't just mean you feel great about yourself or you feel like crap. Maybe a better way to think about it is constructive versus dysfunctional.

So a *constructive* kind of self-talk would be any kind of self-talk that leads you in the right direction, toward your goals and toward becoming a better you.

Dysfunctional self-talk would be any self-talk that bogs you down in unproductive, stale, repetitive patterns, especially if those patterns make you feel miserable and helpless.

It's important to note here that negative emotion (or negative *affect*) is not necessarily your enemy. It's how you *think* about negative emotions that makes them negative. In other words, how you represent negative emotions to yourself in your own self-talk is the key ingredient that turns them into real negativity.

How so? Researchers studying depression have figured out that people with clinical depression have a kind of compulsive destructive self-talk.[1] Psychologists call it *rumination*, and its characteristic is repetitively going over symptoms of distress, like a scab you keep obsessively picking at. Its other characteristic is passivity. You don't focus on solutions but problems.

So you have a negative emotion, such as sadness, but, on top of that sadness, you're telling

---

1 . Papageorgiou, C. & Wells, A. (2004). Nature, functions, and beliefs about depressive rumination. In C. Papageorgiou & A. Wells (Eds.), *Depressive rumination: Nature, theory and treatment* (pp. 3-20). West Sussex, UK: John Wiley & Sons.

yourself this toxic story: *It's all useless, I can't do anything right. I've been stuck in this same position forever and I'll never get out of it.*

Dysfunctional self-talk tells a story. It's the wrong kind of story, a story in which you're passive and helpless.

In *constructive* self-talk, on the other hand, you see yourself as someone who can achieve your goals. That doesn't just lift your mood. It's a self-fulfilling prophecy. If you see yourself as capable, then you have the right perspective to become capable. That puts you in the driver's seat.

With constructive self-talk, you might tell yourself:

You've faced challenges before, and with courage and hard work, you overcame them. And you can overcome this one, too.

You've made mistakes before; it's not the end of the world. Now that you know more, you can use this information to get closer to what you really want.

Your life is pretty good. Sure, there are some improvements you want to make here and there. And you're fully up to the task.

You're good at your job and you should feel proud. You have a right to take credit for a job well done and to feel happy and proud when people praise you.

(You may have noticed the use of the second-person in these examples. There's a reason behind that, which we'll get around to, but, for now, I just wanted to draw your attention to it.)

Exercise II

Keep a journal or notepad with you. Keep two lists titled "Constructive Self-Talk" and "Dysfunctional Self-Talk." Take note of your positive and negative self-talk as you go about your day or your week. Whenever you find yourself engaging in negative self-talk like "I'm always late" or "I suck," write down your thoughts in the dysfunctional list. And whenever you find yourself engaging in positive self-talk (e.g., "I can do this" or "I can nail this presentation"), write down those thoughts, too.

At the end of the day or week, go over your lists. Did you engage more in positive or negative self-talk? How do you *feel* when you read each list? Tally it up and take note of whether or not you have more positive or negative self-talk. If the negative predominates, don't worry, we're going to go over strategies for changing that. And if it's 50/50 or mostly positive, then that's great, but maybe we can make it even better.

I'm deliberately keeping the timeframe flexible here. If you have a very busy schedule, you might not get a chance to make many notes on any single day. So you can stretch the exercise out over a week, or however long it takes to come up with a decent list of ten to twenty items.

Don't skip this exercise and don't throw out your notes because we're going to come back to them later.

Chapter 3 – Impact of Negative Self-Talk

Negative self-talk has a number of unhealthy effects. Obviously, it makes you feel bad about yourself. It's associated with anxiety, depression, stress, low self-esteem, and feelings of vulnerability. But it can also become a self-fulfilling prophecy that harms your performance and even ruins your life. One study found that healthy teenagers of normal weight who just *perceived* themselves as overweight were more likely to become obese later in life.[2] Other research has found that negative self-talk can make your performance worse in everything from academia[3] to your job and can even make you worse at playing darts.[4]

Negative self-talk is especially associated with higher levels of stress and poor emotional regulation when faced with stress. We've all experienced stress, and we know what it's like. But to really understand what's going on with it, we need a tighter definition.

Stress can be understood as a set of physiological responses to something in our environment. The physical symptoms of stress include:

- Muscular tension and pain
- Pain in the upper back, shoulders, and neck
- Elevated heart rate and chest pain
- High blood pressure
- Headache
- Digestive problems such as nausea, diarrhea, constipation, and ulcers
- Low libido, inhibited sexual function or impotence
- Insomnia
- Tightness in the jaw and teeth grinding, especially while asleep
- Sweating

---

[2] . Sutin, A. & Terracciano, A. (2015). Body weight misperception in adolescence and incident obesity in young adulthood. *Psychological Science, 26*(4), 507-511.

[3] . Van Sistine, A. J. (2008). *Negative self-talk in school-aged children* (Unpublished research paper). University of Wisconsin – Stout, Menomonie, WI.

[4] . Van Raalte, J. L., Brewer, B. W., Lewis, B. P., Linder, D. E., Wildman, G., & Kozimor, J. (1995). Cork! The effects of positive and negative self-talk on dart throwing performance. *Journal of Sport Behavior, 18*(1), 50-57.

- Frequent illness (colds and so on) due to weakened immune system

One theory suggests that stress is basically the same as a fight-or-flight response. We evolved fight-or-flight to deal with specific threats on the environment. When our prehistoric ancestors faced a predator in the wild, they would tense up and become extremely alert. Their heart rate would increase. Adrenaline would spike. Their bodies were preparing to either face their foe in a life-or-death struggle or run like hell in the opposite direction.

With agriculture and urbanization, cities, towns, and smaller settlements replaced nature as our primary environment, and society became exponentially more complex. But our brains lagged far behind. We still relied on the same Paleolithic, hunter-gatherer cognitive toolkit for navigating life, but life less and less resembled the environment to which we were best fitted. We no longer rely on hunting and gathering, let alone farming, to sustain us, but on collecting money in exchange for producing valuable services or goods. So anything that threatens our wallets is experienced as a threat to survival. Also, survival was associated with belonging to a tribe. Those who were banished from the tribe soon perished. So, anything that separates us from our circle of family and friends is felt as a threat to survival, even if our wallets are fat.

Nowadays, the threats or stressors in our environment are numerous and constant. You have the possibilities of losing a job, not getting that raise, losing to a competitor, failing a class, losing with investments, committing a humiliating faux pas in a social setting, or being stigmatized by your peers for some mistake.

The problem here is that the fight-or-flight response was adapted to sudden and short-term threats, not gradual and long-term ones. So we react to long-term stressors as if they were short-lived, but they're really not. The physiological responses we have to threats are beneficial in that they give us the energy and quickness to get out of the way of a speeding car, for instance, and then subside. However, if something continually provokes those responses over a long time, they have a negative effect. So, while short-term stress can actually benefit health and longevity, long-term chronic stress causes us to live shorter, less healthy lives.

Negative self-talk increases that stress by distorting our perception of challenges and our ability to meet them. In other words, it makes routine difficulties look like threats. It makes things seem worse than they really are. Thus, it makes stress even more stressful.

It does this in a few ways. We can break them down into a number of broad patterns or *cognitive distortions*.

- **Catastrophizing** – Also known as "making a mountain out of a molehill," catastrophizing refers to making bad situations seem much worse than they are. You didn't just make a mistake; you made an utter fool of yourself. You spilled some milk on the carpet. You'll never get it out; what a disaster!

  Well, not really. Everyone makes mistakes, and spilled milk can be cleaned up.

- **Personalization** – This is also sometimes called personalizing. It means automatically referring everything to yourself, imagining it has something to do with you. Your boss forgot to CC you on an email, so you imagine it's because they're unhappy with your work. In reality, it could have nothing to do with you at all. Beware the trap of thinking too much and over-analyzing the actions of others.

- **Blaming** – You could be blaming yourself or others. If you're blaming others, consider how you may bear some of the responsibility. If you're blaming yourself, consider that not all problems are your fault; you're not in control of everything, so you're only to blame for the things you could have changed. Be forgiving to both yourself and others.

- **Filtering** – This means only considering the negative aspects of something, not the positive ones. Trouble in your relationship? There's a good chance you're focusing on the negative in your partner and forgetting their good side and all the ways they treat you kindly. You have to make a conscious effort to balance your thoughts by thinking of the positive, also.

- **Overgeneralizing** – You fail at something one time, and from that conclude that *you* are a failure who can't get anything right. It's a mistake to think that way, both emotionally and factually. "One" is not a big enough sample size to draw any conclusions. Try proving yourself wrong. Each time you fall down, you learn something you need to know to achieve eventual success.

- **Black-or-white thinking** – Things are either awesome or they suck. I'm either #1 or I'm a failure. Life is a lot more complicated than that. There are many shades of gray. Almost nothing is completely black or white.

This isn't an exhaustive list. There are many other cognitive distortions of this kind, such as *jumping to conclusions* and so on. They're a key tool in clinical paradigms such as cognitive-behavioral therapy. If you're interested in learning more about them—and it's definitely well worth your time—the Wikipedia page for cognitive distortion has a great list.

Right about now, you may be thinking to yourself, *But what if my negative self-talk is true? What if it's accurate to focus on the negative? What if things really are black and white? What if I really am a failure and a loser?*

Well, first of all, "loser" is a value judgment, not a fact. And, yes, value judgments are extremely useful—indeed indispensable—*if* you're trying to decide whether or not to buy something, or whether or not you want to get to know someone, or whether that person you think of as your friend is really a friend who's there for you when you're in need or is just a mooch who's taking advantage of you.

Value judgments are also useful for weighing your own habits, decisions, and actions and deciding whether or not they're good for you and the people you care about, whether they're ethical, and so on.

But value judgments are *worse than useless* when they're global judgments of *yourself*. Because, for better or worse, you're stuck with yourself. And you are the material you have to work with. So, since you can't just reject yourself, it's damaging to beat yourself up. You'll just end up in a rut, feeling hopeless. And that won't be because you were seeing things clearly. It will be because you blinded yourself to the truth.

Or as the highly recommended former trader and risk and probability expert Nassim Taleb put it in his book *Anti-fragile*:

> *A loser is someone who, after making a mistake, doesn't introspect, doesn't exploit it, feels embarrassed and defensive rather than enriched with a new piece of information, and tries to explain why he made the mistake rather than moving on.*

But that's not you, because you're here, reading this book and introspecting. You're thinking about yourself, thinking about *how* you think, working out better strategies for self-talk and living, and enacting them to make positive changes in your life.

The idea is to base everything on facts, not value judgments. Value judgments are only as true as the facts they're based on. So start with what you know about the situation. Get the facts right. Know what you want. And figure out how to get from here to there.

Learned Helplessness

Martin Seligman is a psychologist who did famous research on classical conditioning. He performed an experiment that involved delivering small electrical shocks to dogs. Every time he gave a dog a shock, he would ring a bell. The dogs soon came to expect an electrical shock even when the bell wasn't being rung. (This was in the 60s, so the ethical standards were a bit lax.)

Then he put the dogs in a room divided by a low partition. On one side, the floor was electrified, and on the other side, it wasn't. He put the dogs on the electrified side. Then he delivered a shock to the dogs through the floor.

Now, the partition was low, so the dogs could have jumped over it with ease. But the weird thing was they *didn't even try*. In fact, the dogs would just lie down and accept their senseless punishment with stoic resignation.

He tried the same thing with dogs that hadn't been exposed to any electric shocks. He put them into the same room and delivered a shock through the floor. Those dogs jumped over the partition without hesitation.

It's kind of like how if you leave a horse's reins draped over a post without tying them, the horse will just stand there. Even though the horse could easily wander off, it's used to the idea of being tied up, so it just assumes that it can't go anywhere.

Seligman called this discovery *learned helplessness*. Later research has linked learned helplessness to depression-like symptoms in animals.[5]

It's even more messed up than that, though. People with learned helplessness are not as good at solving problems and have lower relationship and job satisfaction.[6] Learned helplessness is what keeps people in an abusive relationship. It's what keeps some people stuck in poverty even when they have a chance to get out, and it's what prevents some children from even trying to improve their academic performance. Learned helplessness makes you neglect the things in your life that you need to change.

That's because you're constantly telling yourself that you can't change and you can't improve things. Negative self-talk is a symptom of learned helplessness. It's the voice in your head that says *I can't* and *It's no use*.

Do yourself a favor. Consider burning that victim script and completely rewriting it from scratch with positive self-talk.

---

5 . Maier, S. F., & Watkins, L. R. (2005). Stressor controllability and learned helplessness: The roles of the dorsal raphe nucleus, serotonin, and corticotropin-releasing factor. *Neuroscience & Biobehavioral Reviews, 29*(4-5), 829-841.
6 . Henry, P. C. (2005). Life stress, explanatory style, hopelessness, and occupational class. *International Journal of Stress Management, 12*(3), 241–256.

Exercise III

- Write down the categories of negative self-talk in your notebook: Catastrophizing, Personalization, Blaming, Filtering, Overgeneralizing, and Black-or-White Thinking. Leave a bit of space after each one because you're going to be keeping tally.

  Now go back over your notes from the previous exercise. Take the list of negative self-talk and consider each item you wrote down previously. Which category of cognitive distortion does it belong to? For example, if it's catastrophizing, make a score mark under "Catastrophizing." If an item seems to fit more than one category (e.g., both overgeneralizing and black-or-white thinking), go ahead and add a point for both categories.

  At the end, look at your results. You'll probably notice that your negative self-talk tends to fall into one or two of the categories more than others. Those are the areas you want to work on. So if you scored highest in black-or-white thinking, for example, you will want to be on guard for that.

- Whenever you catch yourself in negative self-talk, stop and write it down. Or if you can't write it down, just think about it. But think about it in a systematic way. Ask yourself:

  1. Is this falling into a cognitive distortion, and if so, what kind? Identify the distortion if you can.

  2. What piece of information or aspect of the situation might you be missing that's causing you to perceive things this way?

  3. What would be a more positive, accurate, and empowering way for you to look at it?

You may not have a good sense of how to answer this last one yet, but go ahead and take a stab at it. We'll cover it more specifically in the next chapter.

Learning to be watchful of your thoughts is an incredibly useful habit to have. Pay attention to what's going on in your mind, what kind of thoughts you're having, and what kind of self-talk is going on. And when dysfunctional, distorting self-talk comes up, interrogate it systematically. Then you'll know for yourself whether there's really something behind it or if it's just a puff of smoke.

- Notice how you feel when you're stuck in negative self-talk. Are you happy? Sad? Nervous? Confident? And so on. Write it down. How about your life: Is it keeping you from doing what you're doing? Suppose you had negative self-talk about presenting an idea to your boss. After you talked to yourself that way, did you present your idea or did you back down?

Chapter 4 – Positive Self-Talk

The number one advantage of positive self-talk is that you avoid the downsides of negative self-talk.

That might not sound like a very good deal, but when you think about it, negative self-talk is associated with stress, anxiety, depression, rumination, and low self-esteem. So if you suffer from one, a few, or all of those (and we all do to some degree), imagine *not* having that. Imagine not feeling constantly stressed, overwhelmed, or outmaneuvered and outgunned by life's challenges.

The *absence of the negative* is actually a hidden, silent positive. It leaves no testament of itself, makes no statement. All those bad things that *could* be in your life but *aren't* will never leave a record of their nonexistence. You don't get an email in your inbox every morning that says, "Good news! Your house hasn't burned down, you haven't been swallowed by lava from an erupting volcano, and you also don't suffer from crippling lack of confidence in your decisions."

But it is important to be aware of the absence of the negative. It's important to sometimes think to yourself, "I'm fortunate to have a functioning pair of kidneys." Otherwise, it never occurs to you to appreciate the good things that you have and the bad things that you don't have, until you're already hooked up to a dialysis machine.

Now don't get me wrong. I'm not saying if there's an absence of stress, anxiety, depression, and so on that everything will be rosy and you'll always feel cheerful. You won't. The absence of negative emotion doesn't necessarily mean the presence of positive emotion. But the absence of negative emotion is itself a good thing and worth working toward.

I'm also not saying that if you work on positive self-talk, you'll never experience stress or any negative emotion. You definitely will experience those things on occasion. And, actually, it's good to experience stress *sometimes* because it improves your health and makes you live longer. In fact, if you never experienced any stress at all, it would mean you weren't challenging yourself enough, that you weren't stepping outside of your comfort zone, that you weren't giving your life any of the kind of friction it needed to generate heat, energy, and growth.

Challenge or Threat?

That brings us to the most important difference between positive and negative self-talk:

Negative self-talk views stressors as a threat.

Positive self-talk views stressors as a challenge.

If you're engulfed in negative self-talk, you're robbing yourself of agency in the face of life's suffering and difficulty. You're like the dog that just lies down on the electrified floor and doesn't even try to jump the fence.

If you're harnessing positive self-talk, you're taking authorship of your own being and actively writing your story as its events unfold. You are, moment to moment, claiming your free agency and constantly giving birth to a new self.

There's a way to do that optimally. It's no good to avoid challenges altogether, because then you're basically just a baby. You're not a fully formed human being because you're just living for momentary pleasures and short-term rewards. Two-year-olds do that.

But it's no good either to take on monstrous challenges that overwhelm you because if the challenge is too big, let's face it, you'll probably fail. Then you'll feel like a failure, which will just destroy your confidence and set you up for the next failure. Most of us have some sense of where our limits are and it's easy to imagine things we wouldn't be able to handle. Reconciling general relativity and quantum mechanics? Yeah, probably not going to pull that one off.

You ideally want to hit a sweet spot where you're challenging yourself, but not extremely, so that you have a pretty good shot at winning. But the challenge also has to be hard enough that it forces you to grow and develop your abilities.

Some fine-tuning is involved. Think of it like a guitar string. If you tune it too tightly, the pitch gets higher and higher until it snaps. But if you tune it too loosely, the pitch gets lower and lower until the string just rattles against the frets and sounds like nothing.

Your own emotions are like the sound of the guitar string. They'll tell you if you've got the balance right. When you're facing challenges without pushing yourself too hard and also without being too soft on yourself, you'll feel positive, interested, attentive, and engaged. You'll have a sense that *what you're doing matters*.

But if you're pushing too hard, you'll feel panicky, nervous, overwhelmed, and overstretched. And if you're being too soft, you'll feel boredom at first. And if it gets really bad, a creeping malaise, a crawling emotion of uneasiness, dread, and rot, accompanied by a nagging sensation that you're wasting your life.

So that's how you know when you've hit the sweet spot and when you need to make adjustments. Your mind is an instrument. Be like a musician and tune it often and well.

Self-Leadership

A 2013 study of effective and ineffective senior executives had them write letters to their future selves.[7] The researchers took these letters as indicative of the kind of self-talk the executives had.

They also took effective leadership as predicated on good self-leadership – basically discipline, self-management, and taking challenges that are intrinsically motivating. Self-leadership is

---

7 . Rogelberg, S., Justice, L., Braddy, P. W., Paustian-Underdahl, S. C., Heggestad, E., Shanock, L., Baran, B. E.... Fleenor, J. W. (2013). The executive mind: Leader self-talk, effectiveness, and strain. *Journal of Managerial Psychology, 28*(2), 183-201

pretty much the same as the self-agency we talked about earlier: taking authorship of yourself and your life.

They defined positive or constructive self-talk as "characterized by accurate self-analysis, well-grounded beliefs, and an encouraging orientation" and negative self-talk as "a tendency to focus on and perseverate about the negative aspects of challenging situations."

What they found, of course, is that the effective leaders and, therefore, those who have good *self-leadership,* also exhibited positive self-talk in their writing to themselves. Positive self-talk was further found to have a positive correlation to creativity and problem solving. They wrote letters to their future selves that were motivating, self-compassionate, reflective, and perceptive.

Positive self-talk was connected to stronger leadership qualities and lower job-related stress. Negative self-talk was connected to weaker leadership and lower creativity and problem solving. Whereas managers with negative self-talk saw problems as worrisome obstacles, those with positive self-talk saw them as challenges that contained opportunities.

Self-Deception and False Positivity

At this point, you may have some doubts about positive self-talk. It may seem like it's all about cheerleading for yourself, telling yourself that you can do it, making cheesy self-affirmations, and so on.

Isn't that, well, *bullshit*? Doesn't it sometimes become lying to yourself?

No, actually, and here's why. Positive self-talk is not about telling yourself that you can do things that you can't. It's not about pretending that something is the case when it isn't.

Let's call that the trap of the false positive. Just like a false positive on a diagnostic test, it indicates that something is there when it isn't. You don't want to fall into that trap, because it will make you believe you've achieved something you haven't really achieved. And if you fool yourself into thinking you've already achieved a goal, even though you haven't, then you won't try to achieve it, even though you should.

Consider the following example. You're overweight, you know it, and you don't want to be.

The negative mode of self-talk would say, *I'm so fat* and probably many other adjectives, too: *ugly, unattractive*, etc. It's clearly not good to just heap scorn on yourself, because all it does is make you feel helpless. If you feel helpless, you won't do anything about it.

The false positive mode of self-talk would say, *I'm in perfectly good shape. I don't need to change anything.* But something tugs at your mind from inside. It's the nagging, persistent knowledge that you're fooling yourself. You can't really be satisfied with self-deception because, on some level, in order to lie to yourself, you have to know that you're lying. Because if you don't know that you're lying, you're not lying, you're just wrong.

The *true* positive mode of self-talk would say: *I want to lose ten pounds, and I know what I need to do to achieve it.*

Notice how in the true positive mode of self-talk, you're neither lying to yourself nor are you beating yourself up. You're honestly acknowledging that you're not where you'd like to be. But you're doing so in a way that states where you would like to be *specifically*. And you're also affirming your own ability to get there.

Truly positive people are:

1. *Realistic* about themselves,

2. *Specific* about what they want and how to get it, and

3. *Confident* about their ability to achieve their goals.

Notice how this fits the definition of constructive self-talk offered in the study above: "accurate self-analysis, well-grounded beliefs, and an encouraging orientation."

Examples of Self-Talk

At this point, you get the idea, but it's helpful to look at specific instances. So let's get concrete with some examples that will help bring things into clearer focus.

Negative: *If I speak during this meeting, I might say something dumb and make a fool of myself in front of the higher-ups. I should just stay quiet.*
Positive: *You have interesting and worthwhile ideas to bring to the table. If you share them, the higher-ups can evaluate them for themselves. If they like them, great! If not, no skin off your back. Nothing ventured, nothing gained.*

Negative: *This hobby of mine is just a side thing, really. I'm just an amateur. It would be embarrassing to show the things I make to strangers.*
Positive: *Your non-work interests might be interesting to other people, also. Get your ideas and creations out there and see what happens. You could meet a lot of interesting, like-minded people who help you improve. Hell, maybe you could even turn it into a business! You won't know until you try.*

Negative: *I can't believe he didn't return my phone call. Now I know he's blowing me off and just doesn't respect me.*
Positive: *Maybe something big came up or he's just swamped and couldn't get around to it yet. Who knows? Give it a bit more time before jumping to conclusions.*

Negative: *She's always doing this to me, always bickering about stupid crap. I'm so sick of her pettiness.*
Positive: *Yes, it's super annoying when she overreacts, but let's be real: don't you sometimes overreact too? And overreaction isn't the only thing she does. She also helps out with a lot of things. Maybe you should try talking to her calmly and with sympathy, figuring out what she's upset about, and coming to a solution.*

Negative: *I'm too busy to learn an instrument.*
Positive: *You choose how to allocate your time outside of work. If it's important to you, you can make some time for practice – even if it's only 15 minutes.*

You might notice a couple of things about these examples.

First, they don't really deal in *facts*, although it might feel that way when you're caught up in your own self-talk. But the truth is it's heavily laden with value judgments, not facts. And value judgments are subjective. Instead of asking yourself the question, are these value judgments true, ask yourself the meta-question: Are these value judgments *valuable*? Are they useful? In other words, do they get you anywhere, do they motivate you, and do they help you or hinder you? Some value judgments will be useful and some won't be. Stick to the ones that help you.

Second, the negative self-talk examples frame things in a way that doesn't admit any solutions or forward momentum. The common theme they present is: It's useless, so don't even bother.

But the positive self-talk examples frame things in a way that approaches things in an open-minded manner that allows for creative problem solving. Positive self-talk is curious, action-oriented, and probing; it's interested in feeling out the texture of life and learning how to work with it practically. It frames things, not in a naively optimistic way, but in a realistic cost-benefit analysis. By weighing the pros and cons practically, positive self-talk helps you make better decisions.

To be more precise, the thing distinguishing positive and negative self-talk is not so much the factual content of the thoughts but the interpretation of situations. That interpretation carries an emotional valence, a positive or negative valuation, and an orientation toward action, passive or active, constructive or dysfunctional. It's extremely helpful to remember that most of our thoughts, positive or negative, are subjective. There's no *fact* to them. Since it's not a matter of true or false, the important question about self-talk then is: Is it lifting you up or keeping you down?

***

So, to recap. One of the biggest benefits of positive self-talk is simply the absence of the negative effects of negative self-talk. But positive self-talk also brings its own positive benefits, namely:

- stronger motivation
- readiness to take challenges as opportunities
- a stronger sense of agency and self-mastery
- self-empathy and self-care
- creativity
- better problem-solving skills

Exercise IV

- Take some of the negative self-talk entries from your journal. In the last chapter, you identified which cognitive distortions are most prevalent in your self-talk, so pay more attention to these.

    With each entry, look at it closely. How much of it is fact and how much is value judgment? What would be a better way to frame it that is motivating, encouraging, self-empathic, and focused on creative solutions? Write down this new, more constructive version.

- Keep a running list of negative thoughts whenever you catch them throughout the day and rewrite them in a more positive, constructive way that affirms your agency. Use the three questions from the previous chapter: Is this falling into a cognitive distortion, and, if so, what kind? What are you missing? What would be a more positive, accurate, and empowering way to look at it?

As you make an effort to have more positive self-talk, observe your feelings and actions. Does changing your self-talk change the way you feel? In a good way or a bad way? How about your own behavior? When you speak to yourself positively, are you more or less likely to pursue your goals?

It's good to write this all down, but if you don't have the leisure to do that, just try to work out a more positive version on the fly, in your head. It's a good habit to get into.

Chapter 5 – Pareto: The 80/20 Rule

You might look at your list from Chapter 2, see only negative items, and despair. You might think it's a hopeless case, that you have far too many negative thoughts, and they'll never let you go.

Well, first of all, stop and look at that thought. Is it based on fact? Sure, you might have all or mostly negative thoughts, but that doesn't mean you can't improve yourself. That's not a fact; it's a prediction, and a wrong one with no evidence for it. Tell yourself this instead: *There are a lot of negative thoughts, but no one ever said this would be easy. I can start small and work on the problem slowly. Sooner or later, it will give.*

A really good explanation from economics can demonstrate this point. It's called the Pareto principle. It's a bit abstract; so first, we'll describe the general idea and then get into what it means practically.

The Pareto principle is a general observation about the unequal shape of some distributions. Vilfredo Pareto was an Italian economist who noticed that, during his life, 80% of the land in Italy was owned by just 20% of the population. Conversely, 80% of the population owned just 20% of the land. This 80/20 apportionment is known as the Pareto distribution.

But the really strange thing about this is that the same pattern shows up everywhere. Most quantifiable phenomena having to do with human society and creative endeavors follow a Pareto distribution, so that it can be described generally: 80% of effects come from 20% of causes.

So, in a given economy, roughly 80% of the wealth will belong to 20% of the people most of the time. While the other 80% of the people will own only 20% of wealth. (This explains a lot of income inequality.) If you run a sales team, roughly 20% of the salespeople will close roughly 80% of the sales. And roughly, 20% of your customers will account for roughly 80% of your sales. And roughly, 20% of the products you offer will account for… you guessed it, about

80% of your sales.

But it's not just the human realm that follows the Pareto principle. Vilfredo Pareto got obsessed with this idea and noticed that even in his vegetable garden, 20% of the pea plants produced about 80% of the peas. So it doesn't just apply to outcomes of human activity, but to the natural world, as well.

Another example is Google Scholar. Google Scholar allows you to search for academic articles. Papers with the most citations will turn up at the top of the search results. Well what happened after Google came out with Google Scholar is that it created a Pareto effect, because the top results on Google Scholar tend to gather even more citations, further cementing their place at the top. The bottom results tend to be ignored. And it follows a roughly 80/20 distribution, although it's more extreme in some cases (for example, 90% of humanities papers are never cited at all).[8]

The Pareto principle appears to be an instance of what economists call the Matthew effect, which is named after a quote from Matthew 25:29: "For to everyone who has, more shall be given, and he will have an abundance; but from the one who does not have, even what he does have shall be taken away."

In other words, the rich get richer and the poor get poorer. Those who have some money are able to invest it and gather even more money. Their wealth keeps growing. Those who have less aren't able to use what they have to get more, because their expenses eat most of their income. At the extremely deprived end, people who don't have a decent set of clean clothes and access to hygienic conveniences such as a shower will run into trouble finding even menial work.

As dismal as that sounds, there's a silver lining, because you can put the Matthew effect to work for you.

---

[8] . Remler, D. (2014). Are 90% of academic papers really never cited? Reviewing the literature on academic citations (blog). Retrieved from http://blogs.lse.ac.uk/impactofsocialsciences/ 2014/04/23/academic-papers-citation-rates-remler/

The thing that the Matthew effect or the Pareto distribution shows us is that things naturally take an unequal shape. They naturally tend to *asymmetry*. And that asymmetry appears because of momentum. So, as psychologist Jordan Peterson emphasizes in his talks, if you make an effort to improve yourself just a little bit every day, every improvement will build on the previous one. That will become the basis for the next improvement, until it becomes exponentially easier. It will have a runaway parabolic effect. "For to everyone who has, more shall be given." This doesn't happen by all at once. You don't jump from the 80% to the 20%. Instead, you accumulate before you climb.

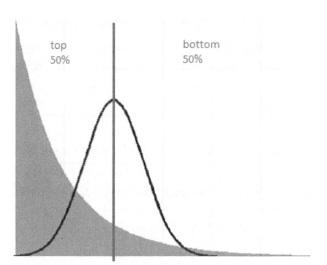

Figure 1: A Normal Distribution (Black) Overlaying a Paretian Distribution (Grey).

I said you accumulate, and, in a certain sense, that accumulation is gradual, but it's effects will be largely invisible until suddenly they're not. That can be seen from the shape of the Pareto distribution in the image above. There's a very small, gradual rise, so gradual that you might not even notice it, like watching a plant grow. Then growth takes off dramatically.

We know from numerous examples that nature doesn't move in continuities so much as in leaps and bounds. Evolution proceeds in punctuated equilibria. Species are pretty stable until a change occurs in the environment, which precipitates a sudden adaptation. At the quantum level, electrons also change states abruptly, the quantum leap. Then, if we zoom back out to the macro level, we see the same thing happening in the stock market. A stock goes sideways, experiencing a period of accumulation, before it suddenly commences an uptrend.

In personal development also, progress occurs in plateaus and steep rises. You have to go through the accumulation period before you experience the uptrend. Eighty percent of people will give up during this stage because there's no visible progress. Without something to show for your efforts, it's easy succumb to doubt and just throw in the towel.

But twenty percent of people will persist through the accumulation phase with a stubborn determination. In the long run, the efforts of determined, disciplined people pay off big time.

Do you want to be part of the eighty percent or the twenty percent?

The good news is that you're moving along the Pareto distribution just by practicing the exercises in this book. Every time you reframe your self-talk in a positive way—in a way that decreases negative emotion, increases positive emotion, builds up your sense of authorship of your life—you are building the staircase, brick by brick, that you will ascend. After a point, the staircase seems to build itself, as if miraculously.

Chapter 6 – Creating the Right Circumstances for Motivation

In the previous chapter, we talked about the cumulative effect of small incremental changes in terms of the Pareto principle, and we talked about the discouraging effect when our progress is sometimes invisible to us.

I want to expand on the latter theme by talking about motivation. Motivation can be strong or weak. And that changes over time. So, a strong motivation can become weak if you start to think you're not getting anywhere with your efforts. And a weak motivation can become strong if you find that something you weren't all that thrilled about surprises you with a reward, whether that's pleasure, money, or whatever.

So the strength of motivation has a lot to do with the expectation of reward but not always. Conviction in an idea or cause can also be very motivating. Sometimes, you labor at something not because you expect a gain from it but because you believe in it. You see it as something that *matters*, part of something bigger than yourself.

Motivation can also be intrinsic or extrinsic. I'll tell you what that means. If you work a normal job, then you show up every morning, give your time and labor to your employer, and get paid regularly. Chances are you wouldn't bother with it if you weren't getting paid. Even if you really enjoy what you do, you're still mainly doing it for an external reward. Hence, extrinsic motivation.

Extrinsic motivation can also be negative: even when you don't feel like going to work, you do it anyway because you don't want the consequences of skipping.

Now, imagine if you volunteer your time at a food bank or homeless shelter. You do it because you want to help people who are in need. You feel compassion for people who are suffering. You feel you *must* do something about it. That's intrinsic motivation.

Or take another example. You spent your whole Saturday playing video games. No one paid you to do that. In fact, you had to buy the system and the games. But you *enjoyed* it; it was *fun*. That's intrinsic motivation.

Generally, intrinsic motivation is stronger because the activity that motivates you is inherently satisfying; the reward is the satisfaction you get. But when you're extrinsically motivated, you have to keep reminding yourself why you're doing something, because the reward and delayed.

But motivation is tricky because it can conflict. So, say you're an avid collector of My Little Pony, or you want to be, but you're afraid of what your friends will think about your hobby. Here you have an intrinsic motivation – your interest in collecting a toy – pitted against an extrinsic motivation – social pressure to fit an established role, namely that of an adult who shouldn't have the same interests as a seven-year-old girl.

So what do you do? Maybe you go to conventions to meet other adult fans of My Little Pony, so you don't feel so isolated, while carefully avoiding disclosing your hobby to others in your social circle, all the while hoping that they never find your cosplay pictures from the convention on social media.

Where this conflict gets really perverse is when you're working on any self-improvement, as you are now by reading this book and trying to change your self-talk. Because you'll quickly find who is your friend and who isn't. Your friends are the ones who support what you're doing and encourage you to make improvements. Now, that doesn't mean that they never question you, but if they're happy when you score a victory and improve yourself, then they're your real friends.

Your fake friends are the ones who display odd emotions whenever you have a victory. Instead of cheering you, they might tell you they're jealous or try to minimize your accomplishment by tearing it down. If you're trying to quit smoking, your smoker "friends" will offer you cigarette. If you're trying to quit drinking, the drinkers will say, "Come on, just one beer!" If you start dating someone new, they'll criticize that person or make you paranoid that he or she is unfaithful.

It may even be subtle. For instance, if you're working on making changes through positive self-talk, they'll notice that your attitude has become more positive and respond by amping up their negative chatter to fill your head with doubt.

So watch out for such people and know who your friends are, especially if you're working on self-improvement. Because when you're trying to go up, there will be people who want to pull you down.

Social pressure isn't all bad, though, and it can be leveraged to improve your motivation. And, let's face it, sometimes we have bad days. Sometimes, it's because something particularly bad happened, or sometimes we're just off.

On those days, all our thoughts are negative and we have no energy to put into being more positive. At those times, it's good to have a true friend around, someone who can lift us up and encourage us when we can't encourage ourselves.

The first trick for leveraging social pressure is to surround yourself with the right people. When you do that, you'll notice that the way you perceive yourself changes.

If you're around negative people, your thinking and self-talk will become negative. You'll see the downside of everything, doubt yourself, question the usefulness of even trying.

If you're around positive people, your self-talk will become positive. Your friends who care about you will encourage you with empathy and give you empowering perspectives, and you'll internalize that in your own thinking and self-talk.

The second trick is to announce your plans to your friends. Say you want to lose weight and are planning to start running three times a week. If they care about you, they'll be interested. The next time they see you, they'll ask something like, "How's the running going?" You'll know they'll ask that but if you don't actually follow through, you'll end up looking bad. So even when you're feeling unmotivated, you think of how bad you'll look if you don't stick to your word. That may just provide the extra push you need when your motivation is weak.

Be aware that social pressure is a double-edged sword. Imagine a novelist who earnestly believes he has at least one great book in him. He's single-mindedly writing year after year, just waiting for his big break: the publishing deal, the helpful agent, winning the Young Lions Fiction Award. Whenever he goes to a family reunion, relatives ask him how the novel is going. But he can just tell from their tone of voice that they're judging him. And even worse, they bring up his rich, successful cousin.

Did you get any publishing deals yet? No? Well, I'm sure something will pan out. Hey, your cousin Todd is doing great in his position at JP Morgan; he just got a big bonus last month. Did you ever think about a career in finance?

You have to have unassailable fortitude to keep up your motivation under such circumstances. So, avoid situations where your motivation may be undermined. Instead, try to bolster your confidence from within. Otherwise, you'll internalize all of that as negative self-talk and end up undermining yourself.

So don't try to swim against the current in your efforts to change your attitude and your life. Select your social environment so that it will be maximally motivating. Then, your mind will naturally follow, and you'll just effortlessly have positive, encouraging, empowering thoughts.

Chapter 7 – The Self

We all have an idea of who we are, an image of the person we believe ourselves to be. In other words, we have an identity. We use the words "I" and "me" all the time without stopping to think about what these actually refer to.

Well, the more philosophical among you may have pondered that question. But for most of us, it never seemed very relevant. Obviously, I am myself, the person speaking. Who else would I be? Case closed.

Not exactly. It turns out to be a bit more complicated than that. We are, after all, animals. We evolved in certain ways. At some point, we picked up the belief in a self, but why? What use does it serve to believe in the self? What is its adaptive function? And how does self-talk relate to that?

If self-talk is an evolutionary phenomenon, it's obviously a human one. After all, self-talk is just an internal form of talk, and talking is something that humans do. So what is the adaptive function of self-talk?

If you cut open your skull and started poking around inside your brain, you wouldn't find anything you could pick out and say, "Aha! There it is, my *self*!"

In fact, efforts by neuroscientists to find a locus for the self in the brain have produced somewhat confusing results. Without getting into the technical details, the picture that emerges from neurology is that of the self as put together from complicated interactions between multiple parts of the brain. .[9]

The point is that the self is a complex idea. Our intuition of the self as unitary perspective, a stable reference point, is an illusion. It's not a single identifiable entity, but a combination of neurological and psychological processes.

[9] . Pfeifer, J. H., Lieberman, M. D., & Dapretto, M. (2007). "I know you are but what am I?!": Neural bases of self- and social knowledge retrieval in children and adults. *Journal of Cognitive Neuroscience, 19*(8), 1323-1337.

From a psychological point of view, the self is connected to self-talk, which internally verbalizes your self-perception, how you view yourself, and also the perception of others and things like stressful events. This is obviously a bit abstract and doesn't seem strictly necessary for survival. But one theory of human intelligence is that it evolved in part so that we could imagine things that aren't actually happening right now.

That's useful because then you can run different scenarios in your head and let them play out without actually having to expose yourself to danger.

If I went bathing in the river right now, how would it turn out? Well, this time of day, there are usually crocodiles. I'd probably get eaten. I should probably stay here in the safety of my hut.

Or a more up-to-date example: If I bought some bitcoin, how would that work out for me? I can imagine big gains and I can imagine big losses. If there were a small probability of doubling or quadrupling my investment, or even getting ten times back, that would be amazing. But I could also lose everything. It could be a complete disaster if I invested all my savings. Well here's what I can do: I'll invest only what I can afford to lose. That would be an acceptable risk for such a big potential payoff.

You get the picture. It's a way of performing thought experiments without actually taking risks.

Imagining future scenarios obviously takes a lot of mental imagery, but it also involves a good deal of talking to yourself in your head. And that conversation is telling a story about you, a person, moving from point A in the past to point B in the future, and how you get there. Point B is where you want to be. It's your goal.

In fact, we already saw that one of the features of positive self-talk is that it empowers you to reach your goals, while negative self-talk impedes you. So we could characterize negative self-talk as self-talk that fails to perform its adaptive function.

Self-talk appears to be a function of two things. One is our ability to run cognitive simulations, and the other is our capacity for language. In order to run these simulations in our imagination, we have to project an image of ourselves, as if we were a video game character.

That requires a separation between one's present, embodied self and the imaginary self. So in a way there's a distance there, as if two selves are running in parallel.

The other side is language. We've evolved a propensity for very sophisticated linguistic communication with other members of our species, and that's turned out to be unbelievably useful. So when you combine these two things together—the distance between your real self and your projected self, and the fact that, as a *homo sapiens*, you're kind of a chatterbox—what you end up doing is talking to yourself.

Now it seems that could also be very useful. Because, just as it's helpful to communicate with other people to get new perspectives and information, it's also incredibly helpful to get some critical self-distance and examine your own perspectives by keeping communication open with yourself. We *think* by talking to others and ourselves.

But self-talk is only as useful as the perspective you're communicating to yourself. If that perspective is disempowering, then it's worse than useless; it's actively harmful. If it's empowering, on the other hand, then you're optimizing its utility.

Chapter 8 – Loving Yourself

You may have noticed something about all the examples of negative self-talk, both your own and the ones in this book. When you're engaging in negative self-talk, you're not doing yourself any favors. You're overly critical of everything; you're shooting down all your own ideas, undermining your confidence, even openly insulting yourself. Just notice the nasty, abusive tone of a lot of negative self-talk.

It's pretty weird. In fact, sometimes, you may even treat yourself the same way someone would treat you if they hated you.

Strangely, just as there are many selfish people in the world, there are also many people who treat others better than they treat themselves. Just think about it. Would you talk to someone you love in the same way you sometimes talk to yourself? Probably not. And if you would, maybe you don't really love that person.

No, if you were talking to someone you really love, you'd be encouraging and supportive. You wouldn't inflate their hopes unrealistically or help them hide unpleasant truths from themselves. But you also wouldn't wither their spirit with constant negativity. You would express that you value their accomplishments and ideas. You would encourage them to work toward the goals that *they* want to work toward and that would make their lives fuller and more meaningful. You would do it with kind, motivating words. And you'd empower them with a perspective that gives them agency and helps them take ownership of their life.

So why in the world wouldn't you do the same thing for yourself?

Whether it's a parent or a spouse, a brother or sister, a relative or close friend, you're also someone who somebody loves, and it would break their heart if they knew that you carry around a voice in your head that disparages you and undermines your life. So perhaps the number one rule for positive self-talk is:

Talk to yourself the way you'd talk to someone you love.

Emotional Intelligence

Emotional intelligence is an idea popularized by Daniel Goleman. Basically, it's the ability to discern your own emotions and the emotions of others and to regulate your emotions. It's also connected to empathy, since empathy allows us both to recognize how others are feeling and to care about it. So with self-empathy or self-love, you will recognize your own feelings and care about your emotional state.

Pretty much the whole program of this book will help you develop your emotional intelligence. For example, learning to recognize the cognitive distortions that characterize negative self-talk, learning how to replace negative self-talk with encouraging self-talk, and so on. In the next chapter, we'll talk about getting to know yourself in terms of personality traits, another key to emotional intelligence. But in this chapter, I just wanted to bring up emotional intelligence in the sense of making friends with yourself by learning how to recognize how you're feeling and to care for yourself as you would a loved one.

If you want to learn more about emotional intelligence, you can find a lot of information in my book on it, Emotional Intelligence Training: A Practical Guide to Making Friends with Your Emotions and Raising Your EQ. It's easily available on the Kindle Store, so give it a read.

Present and Future Selves

You've already heard the Golden Rule a million times: Do unto others as you would have them do unto you. It's a cornerstone of reciprocal ethics that tells you to put yourself in other people's shoes. It tells you to imagine what they want and don't want and to treat them accordingly. Just like you, they want meaning, happiness, and pleasure, and they don't want meaningless suffering.

There's another version of this rule that rarely gets mentioned, and that is: *Do unto your future self as you would do unto your present self.*

How is that a version of the Golden Rule? Well, it just so happens that people tend to think of their future selves as if they were entirely different persons from their present self!

So for example, in one study, Princeton psychologists asked test subjects to choose how much to drink of a repulsive, foul-tasting concoction. Subjects were divided into different groups. In one group, they chose how much they themselves would drink. In a second group, they decided how much the next participant would have to drink. And in the third group, they decided how much they themselves would drink, only two weeks later.

The first group chose to drink a small amount, while the second and third groups chose larger amounts. In other words, when asked to choose much they would drink in two weeks, a person treated their future self the same as if it were a different person.[10]

This goes a long way toward explaining why people tend to go for short-term rewards over long-term payoffs. Why do people procrastinate? Well, that's easy. Procrastination is just avoiding tasks that are presently demanding but will give a reward in the distant future, in favor of activities that give a more immediate reward. And that distant reward is something "someone else" will get, at least the way your brain looks at it.

It's not so surprising when you think about it because "the future" is a relatively high-level abstraction. It might seem pretty basic, but compare that to all other animals. It appears they have only the most rudimentary concept of the future; no creature spends as much time as we do planning and preparing.

The ability to think about the future, on the other hand, is a recent, human-specific adaptation. As we talked about in the previous chapter, it's basically a way of running mental simulations of events that haven't happened. We don't take such cerebral abstractions as

---

[10] . Pronin, E., Olivola, C., & Kennedy, K. (2007). Doing unto future selves as you would do unto others: Psychological distance and decision making. *Personality & Social Psychology Bulletin, 34*(2), 224-236.

seriously as we do the here and now, because they're not *real* . . . yet. And our tendency to seek immediate rewards in the here and now is much older on an evolutionary timescale, hence, basic to our functioning.

"The future" is an artifice of human cognition, a recent graft onto an archaic system. It's like trying to run the latest version of TurboTax on Windows XP. You might get it to work, but it will be slow as hell, function sub-optimally, and you'll be sorely tempted to put off doing your taxes on such a crappy setup and just play Minesweeper instead.

The unfortunate result is that we have an innate cognitive bias to favor short-term rewards over behavior with a distant payoff that may never even materialize.

That's where self-love comes in. An empathetic, loving person will follow the Golden Rule and treat others as they would want to be treated. And a self-loving person will treat their future self the same as their present self. That requires discipline and a conscious effort to counter the innate bias toward the present. But the other side of it is that empathy is a capacity that can be developed. And if you develop your empathy for your future self, you'll have more empathy for others, as well.

Chapter 9 – Getting to Know Yourself

Swimming in the OCEAN

Personality is a big area of research in psychology. The measurement of personality is called *psychometrics*. One of the most well-researched topics in psychometrics is the Big Five personality traits. They are **openness, conscientiousness, extraversion, agreeableness**, and **neuroticism**. An easy way to remember them is the acronym *OCEAN* or *CANOE*.

- **Openness** means a disposition toward novelty. It includes curiosity, imagination, and a drive to learn and discover new things and seek out new experiences. People who score high in openness appreciate the world of art, ideas, and letters. They tend to be more creative and have bigger vocabularies than those who score low in openness. They're also more likely to have unusual, even nutty, beliefs and tend to be politically liberal.

    Those who score low in openness are not interested in novelty and abstraction. They are more pragmatic types interested in "just the facts, ma'am." In the extreme, they can be dogmatic.

- **Conscientiousness** has to do with orderliness and industriousness. People who score high in conscientiousness are tidy, well-organized, disciplined, hard-working, and conventional. They tend to be good planners and have a low tolerance for laziness and poor hygiene in others. They also tend to be politically conservative.

    People who are low in conscientiousness, on the other hand, are messier and not very organized. While they can sometimes be lazy, they are also more flexible and spontaneous.

    It's important to note that conscientiousness and openness are not opposites. One can be both open and conscientious or neither.

- **Extraversion** is an orientation to the outer world of activity and people (as opposed to introversion, which turns inward and prefers less social activities). Extroverts get a lot of energy and positive emotion from engaging with the external. They also tend to be high-energy and very active. When they're around others, they come off as enthusiastic.

    Introverts, by contrast, are less socially involved and prefer quieter activities. This shouldn't be confused with shyness. They don't show their excitement so readily. Introverts also tend to be more independent.

- **Agreeableness** has to do with sensitivity to others' feelings and a desire for harmony and cooperation. Agreeable people get along with others easily and tend to be kind, compassionate, and helpful. Agreeable people are quick to offer compromise. They take the interests of others into account.

    Those who score low in agreeableness are not necessarily jerks. There's a place for disagreeable people, too: they stick to their guns and are not afraid of conflict. They're more self-interested than agreeable people and can veer into being uncooperative and suspicious. But their uncompromising nature can be extremely valuable when it comes time to fight for something important. When you're putting together a team, not everyone can be Bruce Banner. Somebody has to be the Hulk.

- **Neuroticism**, the last trait on the list, is a disposition to unpleasant emotion, especially anxiety, anger, depression, and insecurity. Those who score high in neuroticism are also less emotionally stable and have lower control of their impulses. They have a low tolerance for stress.

    Those who score low on neuroticism are emotionally stable. They have fewer negative emotions, which doesn't necessarily mean they have a lot of *positive* emotions. They just have a higher tolerance for stress and are less likely to experience irritation, depression, vulnerability, anxiety, and so on.

Knowing how you land on the Big Five traits is a must if you're serious about personal development. To be aware of your strengths and weaknesses will help you know yourself. You should also know that while some traits sound negative, they're not necessarily bad. Disagreeableness, for example, kind of sounds like being an asshole. But disagreeable people are brave in a conflict. They don't let others walk all over them. They don't tolerate manipulation and are apt to fight anyone who tries to screw them over.

There's now quite a lot of data on how personality correlates with different areas of life. Conscientiousness, for example, is a major predictor of success in academia and work,[11] consistent across many studies, while neuroticism is a negative predictor.[12]

Okay, but what does all this have to do with self-talk?

Good question. If you're going to work on your self-talk, it's helpful to know about yourself. Then you can target areas of improvement. Half the work of finding solutions is knowing the right way to formulate the problem. And with psychometrics, you have a powerful, empirical, *predictive* tool for doing that.

While there's a lot of evidence that personality is stable over time, there's also plenty of support for the fact that it's subject to change. Some of the change just happens naturally with age. For example, as people get older, they tend to become more conscientious and agreeable and less open, neurotic, and extraverted.[13]

There's also good reason to believe that individuals can change their personality traits at will, provided that they *want to* change and that they make a plan and implement it.[14]

---

11 . Poropat, A. E. (2009). A meta-analysis of the five-factor model of personality and academic performance. *Psychological Bulletin, 135*(2), 322-338.
12 . Trapmann, S., Hell, B., Hirn, J. O. W., & Schuler, H. (2007). Meta-analysis of the relationship between the Big Five and academic success at university. *Zeitschrift Fur Psychologie, 215*(2), 132-151.
13 . Srivastava, S., John, O. P., Gosling, S. D., & Potter, J. (2003). Development of personality in early and middle adulthood: Set like plaster or persistent change? *Journal of Personality and Social Psychology, 84*(5), 1041-1053.

So, to bring this back around, self-talk is the conversation you have with yourself in your head. Paying attention to this conversation can clue you in to patterns of thought and emotion, both constructive and dysfunctional. The Big Five personality traits are dispositions to think, feel, and act in certain ways. Self-talk is part of this bigger picture, and you can alter your self-talk to make changes in how you think, feel, and act.

Neuroticism

For example, if you score high in neuroticism, chances are you have a lot of negative, self-critical self-talk. In fact, *too much* focus on your own self-talk is associated with high neuroticism.[15]

Knowing this is pretty useful. If you're high in neuroticism, then you know that it's probably impeding your performance in your career and whatever goals you have. You also know that while you'll need to improve your own self-talk, too much attention to your self-talk could actually be counterproductive.

So, armed with that knowledge, you know you can benefit from activities that take you out of your head and bring you into your immediate experience. Examples: mindfulness, sports, martial arts, and anything that heightens awareness of your body and your senses. Sometimes, the best way to reform your self-talk is to learn how to change the station and listen to something else. Or just to turn the radio off altogether. More on that later.

Agreeableness

For another example, consider a high score trait agreeableness. You're considerate and caring toward others, but the people in your life may not always have your best interest at heart. So if you're just finding out that you're high in trait agreeableness, this is a good opportunity to reflect on your relationships with other people. Are they as kind and considerate to you as you

---

14 . Hudson, N. W., & Fraley, R. C. (2015). Volitional personality trait change: Can people choose to change their personality traits?. *Journal of Personality and Social Psychology, 109*(3), 490-507.
15 . Poropat, *Meta-Analysis*.

are to them? Do they care about your feelings and interests as you care for theirs? Are they taking advantage of you?

Then you can *pay attention* to what's happening when you're around other people. Especially when there's a conflict between what you want and what they want. Are you just caving to selfish people? And pay particular attention to this: What thoughts are going on in your mind when a conflict comes up? In your self-talk, are you downgrading your own needs?

Observe what's going on in your mind and in your relationships. Then, when you're alone, take some time to think about what your self-talk would sound like if you were more assertive about your best interest.

Research shows that agreeableness is *negatively* correlated with earnings.[16] So disagreeable people actually earn more and get ahead in the workplace. They're seen as tough negotiators. Part of the reason might be that disagreeable employees aren't afraid to ask for more money or threaten to quit. So if you're planning on asking your boss for a raise, you might want to train in some positive, *disagreeable* self-talk such as, *You deserve this promotion, and you're not going to leave that meeting until they give it to you.*

Extraversion

Decreasing your negative self-talk can decrease your negative emotion. But fewer negative emotions doesn't always mean a greater number of positive emotions. Positive emotion is strongly associated with extraversion. There's evidence that this positive emotion comes from more social interaction.[17] So an introvert could also gain more positive emotion by being more socially engaged.

If that's something you want to work on, you could alter your self-talk to give yourself a nudge whenever you're hesitant to jump into a social situation. Tell yourself, *You have something to*

---

[16] . Nyhus, E., & Pons, E. (2004). The effects of personality on earnings. *Journal of Economic Psychology, 26*(3), 363-384.
[17] . Srivastava, S., Angelo, K. M., & Vallereux, S. R. (2008). Extraversion and positive affect: A day reconstruction study of person–environment transactions. *Journal of Research in Personality, 42*(6), 1613-1618.

offer. Put yourself out there. You're fun/interesting/funny and people enjoy your company. The right self-talk can give you more energy and confidence in your social life.

Then you'll create a feedback loop. The more you purposefully nudge yourself into social interactions, the more you'll enjoy them and the easier and more fluid they'll become. Then positive emotion and positive self-talk around your social life will just occur naturally without effort.

Exercise V

- Take a Big Five personality test to find out how you score on each of these traits. If you want a comprehensive test developed by qualified psychologists, you can head over to understandmyself.com. It costs money, though, so if you'd rather not drop the shekels, you can take a quicker and dirtier test at www.psychologytoday.com/tests/personality/big-five-personality-test for free.

- Once you've got your test scores, write them down somewhere. Then do a writing exercise for each of the five traits. Write down a time in your life when that trait served you well and a time when it let you down. For example, if you're low in openness, you can write about a time when your pragmatism helped you and a time when your lack of interest in new things made you miss out on something big. Think about what you could have done to make things turn out differently. Imagine how things could have gone better and write that down too.

- Then take a look at what you've written and identify one or two personality areas you'd like to work on. You might want to improve in all five areas, but for now, stick to two at most and at least one. Come up with some affirmations for improving in that area. These should be short, easy to remember, and powerful. Practice them daily and they'll be there when you need them. In a pinch, you can repeat them to yourself mentally to steer your self-talk in a positive direction. Examples:

"Stand your ground."

"I'm not a doormat."

"Things are better than they look."

"Just breathe."

"There's another perspective on this."

"I'm allowed to express my feelings."

"I have the discipline and will to succeed."

"I'm going to have fun"

"It doesn't matter what other people think; what matters is what I think."

Chapter 10 – Who's Talking?

Most people experience their self-talk as their own voice. When you're engaged in it, you probably think of your inner communication as you talking to yourself. Which you are, kind of. But as we discussed earlier, the "self" that we think of as a unified, continuous "I" is actually more of a complex network of neurological processes. It is like a *community* within one person. According to psychologist Charles Fernyhough, author of *The Voices Within: The History and Science of How We Talk to Ourselves,* "The new science of inner speech tells us that it is anything but a solitary process. Much of the power of self-talk comes from the way it orchestrates a dialogue between different points of view."[18]

If you think about it as being like a computer, the self is not a single identifiable being but a self-organizing cluster of psychological programs. One of these programs activates when you're hungry and is all about procuring food. Another reproduction program activates when you're presented with an alluring mating opportunity. A fight-or-flight program turns on when you're faced with a threat, releasing a cascade of adrenaline into the body that arouses it into a physiological state suitable for fighting a predator or running away really fast.

It's kind of like how the various programs, routines, and subroutines that keep a computer running don't present themselves to view all of the time, but occur in the background. What the end user sees is whatever appears on the screen. But the screen is just a user interface. It's not what's *really* happening under the hood, so to speak, within the circuitry of the motherboard. A computer's user interface is analogous to the experience of a coherent subject or self.

More recently evolved programs have to do with higher cognitive functions, problem solving, narrative formation, and so on. It's only after such processes are well under way that we form this idea that "I" did this: "I" fought or "I" ran away, "I" was turned on. But if you think about it, it's not really like that. And since most of our self-talk is telling this same "I" story, we can see it as a convenient fiction.

[18] . Fernyhough, C. (2017, July 16). Talking to ourselves. *Scientific American, 217,* 76-79.

What if we told ourselves a different, more convenient fiction? One very inconvenient aspect of the current fiction—one big design flaw in the user experience—is the way that negative self-talk appears to be The Self. If you're saying to yourself, *I'm too stupid* or whatever, then the story you're telling is that stupid is <u>what you are</u>. But, fundamentally, that's not what you are. You are as Walt Whitman said:

> *I am large. I contain multitudes.*

Learned helplessness generates negative self-identifications, but this is just a buggy program. Now here's where the computer model breaks down. Because it's not just a simple matter of uninstalling the program. You can't do that because it's an entrenched habit, not so easy to get rid of. But you can do an end-run around the negative self-talk by changing the way you think about it.

Don't think of the negative self-talk as *you*. Think of it as being like a family member you have no choice but to see every holiday, someone irritating but goofy and harmless. Give it a name. Think of it as a foolish, nagging voice that bugs you sometimes. When that unwelcome visitor comes into your head, just tell yourself *Oh, Uncle Vernon is just blathering on and on again.*

The reason this works is that it creates a critical distance between negative self-talk and your identity. When you stop identifying with the inner monologue, especially when it's negative and critical, it loosens its grip on you. It becomes no more important than any other noise.

This is also the principle behind the next chapter.

Exercise VI

Take another look at what you wrote in Chapter 2 when you put your positive and negative self-talk on paper. We're going to be working with what you wrote in the negative self-talk list.

Imagine a character, someone to whom you want to attribute your negative self-talk. It works better if the character is clownish and funny rather than mean or threatening. That way, it's an object of ridicule you can laugh at.

Rewrite each thought or piece of self-talk as if the character had spoken it. What would your reply be if someone said that to you? Write that down, too.

This will give you a jump-start to using the naming technique on the fly in your ongoing inner dialogue. Spend at least some time (a day, two days, or a week) practicing naming your self-talk. Note any changes in how you feel, your level of self-confidence, and your outcomes in areas of your life.

Chapter 11 – What's in a Pronoun?

In the previous chapter, we talked about how identifying your negative self-talk as another person's voice can help create distance from it, so you don't identify it with yourself and get caught up in it.

In this chapter, we'll talk about an easy cognitive hack that allows you to do the same thing from the other side. I'll explain what I mean by that in a bit.

But first, take a minute to think about your own self-talk right now. What pronouns do you usually use? Probably *I, me, my,* and *mine,* which are first-person singular pronouns.

Recent research indicates that it would be much more helpful to use non-first-person pronouns. You could talk to yourself using the second-person pronoun *you* or the third-person *he* or *she*. Or you could just use your own name: *Come on, Julie. You can do it.* Or *Take it easy, Dan. Don't overreact.*

A good example is when LeBron James switched teams in 2010. He famously said at the time, "I didn't want to make an emotional decision. I wanted to do what was best for LeBron James and what LeBron James was going to do to make him happy." It struck many people as a weird way of speaking at the time. They thought he might be a bit soft in the head, jumping from the first to the third person like that.

But thinking and speaking of yourself in the second or third person really does turn out to be a good way to distance yourself emotionally from a situation and make better decisions. And it's supported by solid research.

It works the same way as the previous chapter's trick, by creating distance between yourself and your thoughts. This facilitates emotional regulation and self-control.

Let's break that down. First, non-first-person self-talk helps with self-distancing, also known as de-centering, which means "a process that allows clients to think objectively about irrational thoughts" and helps them to observe their feelings without getting swept away in them.[19]

Furthermore, it eases stress and anxiety in social situations. Two different studies showed that research participants who used non-first-person self-talk had less anxiety and performed better when asked, respectively, to speak publicly and to make a good first impression on a new acquaintance.[20] Other studies showed that non-first-person self-talk allows you to view future stressful situations not as threats, but as challenges that you feel capable of meeting.[21] These studies concluded strongly that non-first-person self-talk is powerful in mitigating anxiety in stressful situations.

Another pair of studies measured the brains of people who were instructed to reflect on negative memories. The control group was told to think about the past with self-talk in the first person, *I* and *me*. The other group was told to reflect on negative memories with non-first-person pronouns. The studies showed that the non-first-person pronoun group had less brain activity associated with emotional reaction while also availing more cognitive control.[22]

This is cutting-edge psychological research that's less than four years old, and it has huge therapeutic potential for helping people take charge of their lives. It's a tremendously useful finding for anyone who's working on personal development because usually self-control takes a lot of practice and effort to overcome emotional reactivity. By talking to yourself in the second or third person, you can actually achieve self-control and emotional regulation with very little effort.

Exercise VII

---

19 . Kross, E., Bruehlman-Senecal, E., Park, J., Burson, A., Dougherty, A., Shablack, H., Bremner, R., Moser, J., & Ayduk, O. (2014). Self-talk as a regulatory mechanism: How you do it matters. *Journal of Personality and Social Psychology, 106*(2), 304-324.
20 . Ibid.
21 . Ibid.
22 . Moser, J. S., Dougherty, A., Mattson, W. I., Katz, B., Moran, T.P., Guevarra, D., Shablack, H., Ayduk, O..., Kross, E. (2017). Third-person self-talk facilitates emotion regulation without engaging cognitive control: Converging evidence from ERP and fMRI. *Scientific Reports, 7*(1), 4519.

As before, take the two lists you wrote down in Chapter 2. This time, rewrite them without using first-person pronouns.

This is a practice round for actually going live with the third-person trick. You guessed it, now we're going to actually practice it for some time. Be LeBron James.

And don't forget to take stock of the results: How does it make you feel? Act? Perform?

Chapter 12 – Turning Down the Volume

We've talked a lot about the downsides of negative self-talk and the upsides of positive self-talk. And while it's extremely important and powerful to work on practicing positive self-talk, it's not always healthy to keep the focus inside yourself. Working on self-talk could become an exercise in navel gazing. Sometimes, it's good to just get out of your head.

That's what I call turning down the volume. It's not really a matter of stopping your thoughts or your self-talk. It's more a matter of deliberately paying attention to something else. An excellent method is meditation, especially mindfulness of the breath.

(If you want to learn more about meditation, I go into much more detail and depth in my other book on mindfulness and success, <u>Mindfulness: The Most Effective Techniques: Connect With Your Inner Self to Reach Your Goals Easily and Peacefully</u>. It's definitely worth reading if you want a practical how-to for mindfulness as a way to live your life. You can find it on the Kindle Store.)

One of the benefits of meditation is that it creates a gap between awareness and thought, between you and your self-talk. That gap is something you can experience as a refreshing, vivid sense of spaciousness. It's worthwhile to practice spending time in spaciousness.

The most immediate reason meditation helps is that it changes your relationship to your thoughts. It allows you to dis-identify with negative self-talk. In meditation, you learn to just let your thoughts be without accepting or rejecting them. So negative self-talk becomes neutral, neither good nor bad, just there. It's just a background noise in your head. Once you relate to it that way, it loses some of its potency to hook you and drag you down.

The other side of it, which you might not expect, is that it also changes the way you relate to positive self-talk. Positive self-talk also becomes neither good nor bad, just part of the background pattern of thought. You don't take it too literally because you're not identifying with it.

This means it becomes harder to fool yourself with false positivity. Even though it creates a kind of "neutral" space, there's an unexpected side to that. Ironically, it makes you much more positive. You begin to cultivate a very genuine, fresh, and natural wellspring of positivity and wholesomeness within yourself. You get to know yourself directly and nakedly without constructing narratives, concepts, and models.

So, to conclude this book, how you talk to yourself is very important, but it's also important to *stop* talking to yourself sometimes. Listen to the silence. Feel the touch of the air on your skin. Feel the warmth of the sun, really see the brightness of the light and the softness of the shade, and experience the rich tapestry of colors, shapes, smells, tastes, and sensations.

And as you transform your negative self-talk into positive self-talk, and then go beyond that into the part of your awareness that isn't talking about the past or future, that's just being in the now, a whole new dimension of life will open up to you.

Good fortune!

Addendum: Specific Applications

Mistakes

Remember that Nassim Taleb quote from earlier? "A loser is someone who, after making a mistake, doesn't introspect, doesn't exploit it, feels embarrassed and defensive rather than enriched with a new piece of information, and tries to explain why he made the mistake rather than moving on."

It's a variation of something you've already heard a thousand times: Learn from your mistakes. You've probably heard it so often you've become immune to it.

Except that it's true and there's a lot of value in restating the obvious. If you don't ever remind yourself of the obvious, you forget it, and it turns out that it's pretty important not to overlook the obvious.

This is a process, and you're going to make mistakes. That's okay. It's better than okay, it's very valuable. Don't look at your mistakes as a personal failure. Look at them as important feedback from your environment. Each mistake contains information that will help you adjust your approach before you try again.

So go ahead and make mistakes, gather information from them, tweak your methods, try again, make mistakes again, rinse, repeat, until you get it right. Then keep doing *that* to make sure you really did get it right and it wasn't just a fluke. There's a word for this methodology. It's called *science*.

Inculcate this attitude. Make it the way you talk to yourself. *Okay, so that didn't work, why not? Maybe it's because you didn't use enough of this. Okay, adjust that and try again.* Recipe for success.

With each mistake, ask yourself, *What can you learn from this? What information does this give you? Okay, that's one interpretation. Can you think of any other interpretations for why things went wrong? Okay, now you have a couple of ideas. How can you do things differently? Try that and see.*

Health and Exercise

We talked about this before in the motivation chapter. Like it or not, we humans are status-seeking animals. And the judgments other people make of us can be incredibly motivating, for better or for worse. Hopefully for better, but that depends on how you select your environment.

If your goal is fitness. You want to eat healthy, exercise, lose weight, get toned. Great.

Now let's imagine two scenarios.

First, you buy equipment and keep it in your home. You're motivated enough to get on the rowing machine every day. But since you're alone in your basement, no one is there to see you get tired after three minutes, clamber off the machine, huffing and puffing, and go sit on the sofa.

Scenario number two is you get a gym membership and start going to the gym several times a week. You see the same people again and again and start getting friendly with them. You're on the Stairmaster, pumping away, and feeling pretty tired, like you might give up. But you're also keenly aware of the very fit, very attractive person of your preferred gender on the Stairmaster next to you. You don't want to look bad in front of him or her, so you push yourself harder and break through your resistance to complete a nice workout.

As we discussed earlier, you contain multitudes. One part of you is the motivation that wants to strive toward a distant goal (delayed gratification) and that part of you is willing to put up with some short-term deprivation, going on a diet, in return for the long-term prospect of improving your health and looking better.

Then there's another part of you that just wants to say, "Screw it" and tear into a bacon double quarter-pounder with cheese.

Then there's another part of you that just wants to plop down on the sofa and go through five straight episodes of *Punisher* on Netflix when you've already scheduled this time for the gym.

But there's also a part of you that wants the approval and good opinion of your fellow humans, and if you know that's motivating you, you can use it to your advantage.

Self-talk can help you with your goals, but it will be a lot easier to work on your self-talk if you set up the right kind of incentives in your environment.

But you also need the self-talk part of the equation. You need an inner dialogue that doesn't say, *This is so heavy; I'm going to drop it* but tells you, instead, *You can do this, just one more rep! Okay, now another rep!*

Not *Oh God, I'm so tired* but *This isn't so bad; in fact, it's kind of invigorating and you're really liking the dopamine. You've got at least another mile in you.*

Wealth and Career

Wealth is a tricky area of human life because it's so tied up with status, and we status-seeking animals care a lot about where we end up in the pecking order.

So, when you don't have wealth, you're likely to be all too conscious of your low relative status. And you're also likely to suffer from the low self-esteem that goes hand-in-hand with negative self-talk. That just further cements your position by discouraging you from changing it. You need a certain amount of confidence and motivation to change, which you won't have if you're stuck in the vicious cycle of feeling lousy about yourself.

The thing about our perception of status is that it's based on relative, not absolute reference points. So a multimillionaire who rubs shoulders with billionaires will feel the sting of low relative status. Put that guy in the same room with a bunch of rich people who are, nevertheless, not as rich as him, and he'll be feeling pretty good about himself.

This is another area where selecting your social environment can be useful. But you want to get it right. You don't want to select an environment where you're the top dog and nobody is better than you at anything, because then you'll never feel the need to challenge yourself. But you don't want to end up in an environment where you're at the bottom of the pyramid, either, because then you'll just feel defeated all the time.

So, try to be around people of similar, though not exactly the same, ability and status as you, with some error around the margins. Then learn everything you can from those people to better yourself.

One way you can work on this with self-talk is to make a point to remind yourself of everything you have whenever you're thinking of what you lack. You might have a really great house or flat, nice furniture, fashionable clothes, a decent paycheck, etc. It doesn't have to be a rich and sumptuous situation, but you should still take the time to appreciate and feel glad for the wealth that you *do* have. Chances are, it could be worse; it could be a lot worse. And if you doubt that, just take a drive through a poor neighborhood.

Maybe all you have is a sound mind and a body in good health. Well, those are assets. You're going to need that intelligence and health to acquire wealth.

You should introspect about how to get to your wealth goals. Maybe you're just looking for a raise. Then you have to tell yourself, *You've been working hard, your results are great, and that deserves a reward. You're going to go into that office with your back straight and head held high. And you're going to convince your boss of what you already know, that you deserve that raise.*

Or maybe you're thinking of starting a business. That can be a daunting leap to make, and you'll need some self-confidence. *You have the brains and the business sense to do this. You* have a good idea for a business and it has a good chance of success. So what are you waiting for? Set some concrete goals, make a plan XYZ of what you need to do to reach them, and go for it!

Or maybe you're trying to figure out why you're not getting ahead in your career. There's a right way and a wrong way to think about that.

Here's an example of the wrong way: *The game is rigged against me. I can't get ahead in this environment because I'm not invited to the club.*

Instead, think about what is required for success. One thing is intelligence. Two other important predictors are conscientiousness and agreeableness, as we talked about earlier. Try to figure out if you need to work on one of these things. Maybe you're not being assertive in trying to get a promotion or a better job; maybe you're not selling your achievements confidently. You have to tell yourself, *It's okay to be disagreeable sometimes. You have to fight to get ahead. You can be assertive without being aggressive and off-putting.*

Relationships

If you're on the dating scene, you have to have confidence. Don't think that only the other person is sizing you up. You're also sizing them up, and rejection is part of the process. So instead of thinking: *How's my hair? Is this shirt too loose? God, that pimple on my nose is so ugly. I can't believe I just told that joke; it's so lame. She/he is just pretending to laugh, what an embarrassment.*

Think of it this way: *You've got a lot of things going for you. You're good-looking, smart, witty, have a lot of interesting things to say, have good manners, know how to treat people with respect, have a strong personal ethic, have a good job,* etc. Think about all the categories in which you've got it going on. *You're the buyer, not the seller in this market. You can afford to be choosy.*

Then tell yourself, *If they don't appreciate all that, there's someone out there who does.*

You're much more interested in the person who does.

Of course, there's a lot more to successful dating than that, but the right kind of self-talk really sets the right tone and helps you bring an attractive confidence. It also helps you bounce back from painful episodes.

If you're in an established relationship, there are only two possibilities: you're with someone who treats you well or you're with someone who doesn't treat you well. If it's the latter, don't hesitate to leave them. Don't tell yourself that you don't deserve better, or that you can't find anyone, or that you'll be lonely.

Instead, tell yourself that you have a lot to offer and you have to be kind to yourself, also, not just to the other person. You owe it to yourself to leave anyone who doesn't respect you.

If you're in a relationship that's going well, however, well, then fantastic! It's pretty easy to be positive about that. *I'm lucky to be with him/her. Sure, we have a disagreement sometimes, but they really make me feel happy and cherished. And they're always there for me in the hard times.*

But remember, the most important relationship is the one you have with yourself. So talk to yourself the same way you talk to the person you love.

<u>One last thing before you go – Can I ask you a favor? I need your help!</u> If you like this book, could you please share your experience on Amazon and write an honest review? It will be just one minute for you (I will be happy even with one sentence!), but a GREAT help for me and definitely good Karma ☺. Since I'm not a well-established author and I don't have powerful people and big publishing companies supporting me, <u>I read every single review and jump around with joy like a little kid every time my readers comment on my books and give me their honest feedback!</u> If I was able to inspire you in any way, please let me know! It will also help me get my books in front of more people looking for new ideas and useful knowledge.

If you did not enjoy the book or had a problem with it, please don't hesitate to contact me at <u>contact@mindfulnessforsuccess.com</u> **and tell me how I can improve it to provide more value and more knowledge to my readers.** I'm constantly working on my books to make them better and more helpful.

Thank you and good luck! I believe in you and I wish you all the best on your new journey!

Your friend,

Ian

Don't hesitate to visit:
-My Blog: www.mindfulnessforsuccess.com
-My Facebook fanpage: https://www.facebook.com/mindfulnessforsuccess
-My Instagram profile: https://instagram.com/mindfulnessforsuccess
-My Amazon profile: amazon.com/author/iantuhovsky

My Free Gift to You – <u>Get One of My Audiobooks For Free!</u>

If you've never created an account on Audible (the biggest audiobook store in the world), **<u>you can claim one free</u> audiobook <u>of mine</u>**!

It's a simple process:

1. Pick one of my audiobooks on Audible:

http://www.audible.com/search?advsearchKeywords=Ian+Tuhovsky

2. Once you choose a book and open its detail page, click the orange button "Free with 30-Day Trial Membership."

3. Follow the instructions to create your account and download your first free audiobook.

Note that you are NOT obligated to continue after your free trial expires. You can cancel your free trial easily anytime and you won't be charged at all.

Also, if you haven't downloaded your free book already:

Discover How to Get Rid of Stress & Anxiety and Reach Inner Peace in 20 Days or Less!

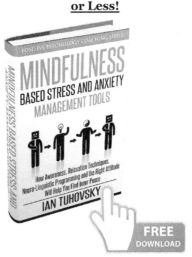

To help speed up your personal transformation, I have prepared a special gift for you!
Download my full, 120 page e-book "Mindfulness Based Stress and Anxiety Management Tools" for free by clicking here.
Link:
tinyurl.com/mindfulnessgift

Hey there like-minded friends, let's get connected!

Don't hesitate to visit:
-My Blog: www.mindfulnessforsuccess.com
-My Facebook fanpage: https://www.facebook.com/mindfulnessforsuccess
-My Instagram profile: https://instagram.com/mindfulnessforsuccess
-My Amazon profile: amazon.com/author/iantuhovsky

Recommended Reading for You

If you are interested in Self-Development, Psychology, Social Dynamics, PR, Soft Skills, Spirituality and related topics, you might be interested in previewing or downloading my other books:

Communication Skills Training: A Practical Guide to Improving Your Social Intelligence, Presentation, Persuasion and Public Speaking

Do You Know How To Communicate With People Effectively, Avoid Conflicts and Get What You Want From Life?

...It's not only about what you say, but also about WHEN, WHY and HOW you say it.

Do The Things You Usually Say Help You, Or Maybe Hold You Back?

Have you ever considered **how many times you intuitively felt that maybe you lost something important or crucial, simply because you unwittingly said or did something, which put somebody off?** Maybe it was a misfortunate word, bad formulation, inappropriate joke, forgotten name, huge misinterpretation, awkward conversation or a strange tone of your voice?
Maybe you assumed that you knew exactly what a particular concept meant for another person and you stopped asking questions?
Maybe you could not listen carefully or could not stay silent for a moment? **How many times have you wanted to achieve something, negotiate better terms, or ask for a promotion and failed miserably?**

It's time to put that to an end with the help of this book.

Lack of communication skills is exactly what ruins most peoples' lives.
If you don't know how to communicate properly, you are going to have problems both in your intimate and family relationships.

You are going to be ineffective in work and business situations. It's going to be troublesome managing employees or getting what you want from your boss or your clients on a daily basis.

Overall, **effective communication is like an engine oil which makes your life run smoothly, getting you wherever you want to be.** There are very few areas in life in which you can succeed in the long run without this crucial skill.

What Will You Learn With This Book?

-What Are The **Most Common Communication Obstacles** Between People And How To Avoid Them
-How To Express Anger And Avoid Conflicts
-What Are **The Most 8 Important Questions You Should Ask Yourself** If You Want To Be An Effective Communicator?
-**5 Most Basic and Crucial** Conversational Fixes
-How To Deal With Difficult and Toxic People
-Phrases to **Purge from Your Dictionary** (And What to Substitute Them With)
-The Subtle Art of **Giving and Receiving Feedback**
-Rapport, the **Art of Excellent Communication**
-How to Use Metaphors to **Communicate Better** And **Connect With People**
-What Metaprograms and Meta Models Are and How Exactly To Make Use of Them To **Become A Polished Communicator**
-How To Read Faces and **How to Effectively Predict Future Behaviors**
-How to Finally Start **Remembering Names**
-How to Have a Great Public Presentation
-How To Create Your Own **Unique Personality** in Business (and Everyday Life)
-Effective Networking

Direct link to Amazon Kindle Store: https://tinyurl.com/IanCommSkillsKindle

Paperback version on Createspace:

http://tinyurl.com/iancommunicationpaperback

The Science of Effective Communication: Improve Your Social Skills and Small Talk, Develop Charisma and Learn How to Talk to Anyone

Discover the powerful way to transform your relationships with friends, loved ones, and even co-workers, with proven strategies that you can put to work immediately on improving the way you communicate with anyone in any

environment.

From climbing the career ladder to making new friends, making the most of social situations, and even finding that special someone, communication is the powerful tool at your disposal to help you achieve the success you truly deserve.

In <u>The Science of Effective Communication</u>, you'll learn how to develop and polish that tool so that no matter who you are, where you go, or what you do, you'll make an impact on everyone you meet for all the right reasons.

Discover the Secrets Used By the World's Most Effective Communicators

We all know that one person who positively lights up any room they walk into, who seem to get on with everyone they meet and who lead a blessed life as a result.

Yet here's something you may not know:

Those people aren't blessed with a skill that is off-limits to the rest of us.

You too can learn the very same techniques used by everyone from Tony Robbins to Evan Carmichael to that one guy in your office who everyone loves, and put them to work in getting what you want - without bulldozing over everyone in your path.

Step-by-Step Instructions to Supercharge Your Social Confidence

<u>The Science of Effective Communication</u> is a fascinating, practical guide to making communication your true super power, packed with expert advice and easy-to-follow instructions on how to:

- Retrain your brain to develop powerful listening skills that will help you build better relationships with anyone and gain more value from your conversations.
- Make your voice more attractive to potential romantic partners.
- Mend broken relationships with family members, partners, and even work colleagues.
- Get your views heard by those in authority without being disrespectful.
- Thrive in any job interview and get that dream job.

Your Complete Manual for Building Better Relationships With Everyone You Meet

Bursting with actionable steps you can use IMMEDIATELY to transform the way you communicate, this compelling, highly effective book serves as your comprehensive guide to better communication, revealing exclusive tips to help you:

- Overcome 'Outsider Syndrome,' make friends, and flourish in any social situation
- Keep conversations flowing with anyone

- Make long-distance relationships not only work, but positively prosper
- Reap huge rewards from a digital detox

And much, much more.

Direct Buy Link to Amazon Kindle Store:
http://getbook.at/EffectiveCommunication

Paperback version on Createspace: http://getbook.at/EffectiveCommPaper

Emotional Intelligence Training: A Practical Guide to Making Friends with Your Emotions and Raising Your EQ

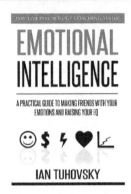

Do you believe your life would be healthier, happier and even better, if you had more practical strategies to regulate your own emotions?
Most people agree with that.
Or, more importantly:
Do you believe you'd be healthier and happier if everyone who you live with had the strategies to regulate their emotions?

...Right?

The truth is not too many people actually realize what EQ is really all about and what causes its popularity to grow constantly.

Scientific research conducted by many American and European universities prove that the **"common" intelligence responses account for less than 20% of our life achievements and successes, while the other over 80% depends on emotional intelligence.** To put it roughly: **either you are emotionally intelligent, or you're doomed to mediocrity, at best.**
As opposed to the popular image, emotionally intelligent people are not the ones who react

impulsively and spontaneously, or who act lively and fiery in all types of social environments. Emotionally intelligent people are open to new experiences, can show feelings adequate to the situation, either good or bad, and find it easy to socialize with other people and establish new contacts. They handle stress well, say "no" easily, realistically assess the achievements of themselves or others and are not afraid of constructive criticism and taking calculated risks. **They are the people of success.** Unfortunately, this perfect model of an emotionally intelligent person is extremely rare in our modern times.

Sadly, nowadays, **the amount of emotional problems in the world is increasing at an alarming rate.** We are getting richer, but less and less happy. Depression, suicide, relationship breakdowns, loneliness of choice, fear of closeness, addictions—this is clear evidence that we are getting increasingly worse when it comes to dealing with our emotions.
Emotional intelligence is a SKILL, and can be learned through constant practice and training, just like riding a bike or swimming!

This book is stuffed with lots of effective exercises, helpful info and practical ideas.
Every chapter covers different areas of emotional intelligence and shows you, **step by step,** what exactly you can do to **develop your EQ** and become the **better version of yourself.**
I will show you how freeing yourself from the domination of left-sided brain thinking can contribute to your inner transformation—**the emotional revolution that will help you redefine who you are and what you really want from life!**

<u>**In This Book I'll Show You:**</u>

- What Is Emotional Intelligence and What Does EQ Consist of?
- How to **Observe and Express** Your Emotions
- How to **Release Negative Emotions** and **Empower the Positive Ones**
- How to Deal with Your **Internal Dialogues**
- How to **Deal with the Past**
- **How to Forgive** Yourself and How to Forgive Others
- How to Free Yourself from **Other People's Opinions and Judgments**
- What Are "Submodalities" and How Exactly You Can Use Them to **Empower Yourself** and **Get Rid of Stress**
- The Nine Things You Need to **Stop Doing to Yourself**
- How to Examine Your Thoughts
- **Internal Conflicts** Troubleshooting Technique
- The Lost Art of Asking Yourself the Right Questions and **Discovering Your True Self!**
- How to Create Rich Visualizations
- LOTS of practical exercises from the mighty arsenal of psychology, family therapy, NLP etc.
- **And many, many more!**

Direct Buy Link to Amazon Kindle Store:
https://tinyurl.com/IanEQTrainingKindle
Paperback version on Createspace: https://tinyurl.com/ianEQpaperback

Self-Discipline: Mental Toughness Mindset: Increase Your Grit and Focus to Become a Highly Productive (and Peaceful!) Person

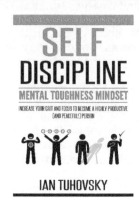

This Mindset and Exercises Will Help You Build Everlasting Self-Discipline and Unbeatable Willpower

Imagine that you have this rare kind of power that enables you to maintain iron resolve, crystal clarity, and everyday focus to gradually realize all of your dreams by consistently ticking one goal after another off your to-do list.

Way too often, people and their minds don't really play in one team.

Wouldn't that be profoundly life-changing to utilize that power to make the best partners with your brain?

This rare kind of power is a mindset. The way you think, the way you perceive and handle both the world around you and your inner reality, will ultimately determine the quality of your life.

A single shift in your perception can trigger meaningful results.

Life can be tough. Whenever we turn, there are obstacles blocking our way. Some are caused by our environment, and some by ourselves. Yet, we all know people who are able to overcome them consistently, and, simply speaking, become successful. And stay there!

What really elevates a regular Joe or Jane to superhero status is the laser-sharp focus, perseverance, and the ability to keep on going when everyone else would have quit.
I have, for a long time, studied the lives of the most disciplined people on this planet. In this book, you are going to learn their secrets.
No matter if your goals are financial, sport, relationship, or habit-changing oriented, this book covers it all.

Today, I want to share with you the science-based insights and field-tested methods that have helped me, my friends, and my clients change their lives and become real-life go-getters.

Here are some of the things you will learn from this book:

• **What the "positive thinking trap" means,** and how exactly should you use the power of positivity to actually help yourself instead of holding yourself back?
• What truly makes us happy and how does that relate to success? Is it money? Social position? Friends, family? Health? **No. There's actually something bigger, deeper, and much more fundamental behind our happiness.** You will be surprised to find out what the factor that ultimately drives us and keeps us going is, and this discovery can greatly improve your life.
• **Why our Western perception of both happiness and success are fundamentally wrong**, and how those misperceptions can kill your chances of succeeding?
• **Why relying on willpower and motivation is a very bad idea, and what to hold on to instead?** This is as important as using only the best gasoline in a top-grade sports car. Fill its engine with a moped fuel and keep the engine oil level low, and it won't get far. Your mind is this sports car engine. I will show you where to get this quality fuel from.
• **You will learn what the common denominator of the most successful and disciplined people on this planet is** – Navy SEALS and other special forces, Shaolin monks, top performing CEOs and Athletes, they, in fact, have a lot in common. I studied their lives for a long time, and now, it's time to share this knowledge with you.
• Why your entire life can be viewed as a piece of training, and **what are the rules of this training?**
• What the XX-th century Russian Nobel-Prize winner and long-forgotten genius Japanese psychotherapist **can teach you about the importance of your emotions and utilizing them correctly in your quest to becoming a self-disciplined and a peaceful person?**
• How modern science can help you **overcome temptation and empower your will**, and why following strict and inconvenient diets or regimens can actually help you achieve your goals in the end?
• How can you win by failing and **why giving up on some of your goals can actually be a good thing?**
• How do we often become **our own biggest enemies** in achieving our goals and how to finally change it?
• How to **maintain** your success once you achieve it?

Direct Buy Link to Amazon Kindle Store:
http://tinyurl.com/IanMentalToughness
Paperback version on Createspace: http://tinyurl.com/IanMTPaperback

Accelerated Learning: The Most Effective Techniques: How to Learn Fast, Improve Memory, Save Your Time and Be Successful

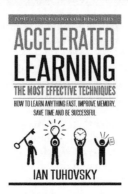

Unleash the awesome power of your brain to achieve your true potential, learn anything, and enjoy greater success than you ever thought possible.

Packed with proven methods that help you significantly improve your memory and develop simple-yet-powerful learning methods, <u>Accelerated Learning: The Most Effective Techniques</u> is the only brain training manual you'll ever need to master new skills, become an expert in any subject, and achieve your goals, whatever they may be.

Easy Step-by-Step Instructions Anyone Can Use Immediately

•Student preparing for crucial exams?

•Parent looking to better understand, encourage, and support your child's learning?

•Career professional hoping to develop new skills to land that dream job?

Whoever you are and whatever your reason for wanting to improve your memory, <u>Accelerated Learning: The Most Effective Techniques</u> will show you exactly how to do it with simple, actionable tasks that you can use to help you:

•Destroy your misconceptions that learning is difficult - leaving you free to fairly pursue your biggest passions.

•Stop procrastinating forever, eliminate distractions entirely, and supercharge your focus, no matter what the task at hand.

•Cut the amount of time it takes you to study effectively and enjoy more time away from your textbooks.

- Give yourself the best chance of success by creating your own optimal learning environment.

Everything you'll learn in this book can be implemented immediately regardless of your academic background, age, or circumstances, so no matter who you are, you can start changing your life for the better RIGHT NOW.

Take control of your future with life-changing learning skills.

<u>Self-doubt is often one of the biggest barriers people face in realizing their full potential and enjoying true success.</u>

In <u>Accelerated Learning: The Most Effective Techniques</u>, you'll not only find out how to overcome that self-doubt, but also how to thrive in any learning environment with scientifically-proven tools and techniques.

You'll also discover:
- How to use an ancient Roman method for flawless memorization of long speeches and complex information

- The secret to never forgetting anyone's name ever again.

- The easy way to learn an entirely new language, no matter how complex.

- The reason why flashcards, mind maps, and mnemonic devices haven't worked for you in the past - and how to change that.

- The simple speed-reading techniques you can use to absorb information faster.

- How to cut the amount of time it takes you to study effectively and enjoy more time away from your textbooks.

- The truth about binaural beats and whether they can help you focus.

- How to effectively cram any exam (in case of emergencies!).

And much more!

Direct Buy Link to Amazon Kindle Store:
http://getbook.at/AcceleratedLearning

Paperback version on Createspace:

http://getbook.at/AcceleratedLearningPaperback

Empath: An Empowering Book for the Highly Sensitive Person on Utilizing Your Unique Ability and Maximizing Your Human Potential

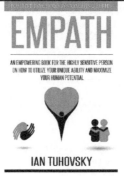

Have others ever told you to "stop being so sensitive?" Have you ever looked at other people and wondered how they manage to get through the day without noticing the suffering going on all around them?

Do you feel so emotionally delicate in comparison to your peers that you have tried to block out what is going on around you? You may have even resorted to coping mechanisms such as overeating, overworking, or smoking as a means of managing your emotions.

Maybe you have tried to "grow a thicker skin," or attempted to cover up your feelings with humor? Perhaps you have always felt different to others since childhood, but could never quite put your finger on why.

If this description resonates with you, congratulations! You may well be an Empath. **Unfortunately, an Empath who lacks insight into their own nature is likely to be miserable.**

Most of us are familiar with the concept of empathy. Aside from sociopaths, who are largely incapable of appreciating what another individual may be feeling, humans are generally able to understand what others are going through in most situations.
Empaths, however, constitute the small group of people who not only understand the emotions of others, but literally feel them too.

In short, an Empath takes this common human ability of relating to other peoples' emotions to extremes.

If you have no idea why you are so readily affected by the emotions of others and the events around you, you will become psychologically unstable. You will be unsure as to where your true feelings end, and those of other people begin.

Hypersensitivity can be a burden if not properly managed, which is why it's so important that all Empaths learn to harness the special gift they have been given.
That's where this book comes in. Millions of other people around the world share your gifts

and lead happy, fulfilling lives. Make no mistake – the world needs us.

It's time to learn how to put your rare gift to use, maximize your human potential, and thrive in life!

If you think you (or anyone around you) might be an Empath or the Highly Sensitive Person – this book is written for you.

What you will learn from this book:
-**What it really means to be an Empath** and the science behind the "Empath" and "the Highly Sensitive Person" classification. Find out how our brains work and why some people are way more sensitive than others.
-**What are the upsides of being an Empath** – find your strengths and thrive while making the most of your potential and providing value to this world (it NEEDS Empaths!) by making it a better place.
-**What are the usual problems that sensitive people struggle** with – overcome them by lessening the impact that other people's emotions and actions have on you, while still being truthful to your true nature, and learn how to take care of your mental health.
-**The great importance of becoming an emotionally intelligent person** – learn what EQ is and how you can actively develop it to become much more peaceful, effective, and a happy person. Discover the strategies that will help you stay balanced and be much more immune to the everyday struggles.
-**The workplace and career choices** – realize what you should be aware of and find how to make sure you don't stumble into the most common problems that sensitive people often fall prey to.
-**How to effectively handle conflicts, negative people, and toxic** relationships – since sensitive people are more much more immune to difficult relations and often become an easy target for those who tend to take advantage of others – it's time to put this to an end with this book.
-**How to deal with Empaths and Highly Sensitive People as a non-Empath** and what to focus on if you think that your kid might fall under this classification.
-**How to connect with other Empaths**, what is the importance of gender in this context, and how to stay in harmony with your environment – **you will learn all of this and more from this book!**

Direct Buy Link to Amazon Kindle Store:
http://tinyurl.com/IanEmpathKindle

Paperback version on Createspace:
http://tinyurl.com/IanEmpathPaperback

Confidence: Your Practical Training: How to Develop Healthy Self Esteem and Deep Self Confidence to Be Successful and Become True Friends with Yourself

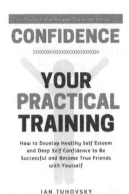

Have you ever considered how many opportunities you have missed and how many chances you have wasted by lacking self-confidence when you need it most?
Have you ever given up on your plans, important goals, and dreams not because you just decided to focus on something else, but simply because you were too SCARED or hesitant to even start, or stick up to the plan and keep going?

Are you afraid of starting your own business or asking for a promotion? Petrified of public speaking, socializing, dating, taking up new hobbies, or going to job interviews?

Can you imagine how amazing and relieving it would feel to finally obtain all the self-esteem needed to accomplish things you've always wanted to achieve in your life?

Finally, have you ever found yourself in a situation where you simply couldn't understand **WHY you acted in a certain way**, or why you kept holding yourself back and feeling all the bad emotions, instead of just going for what's the most important to you?

Due to early social conditioning and many other influences, most people on this planet are already familiar with all these feelings.

WAY TOO FAMILIAR!

I know how it feels, too. I was in the same exact place.

And then, I found the way!
It's high time you did something about it too because, truth be told, self-confident people just have it way easier in every single aspect of life!

From becoming your own boss or succeeding in your career, through dating and socializing, to starting new hobbies, standing up for yourself or maybe finally packing your suitcase and going on this Asia trip you promised yourself decades ago... All too often, people fail in these quests as they aren't equipped with the natural and lasting self-confidence to deal with them in a proper way.

Confidence is not useful only in everyday life and casual situations. Do you really want to fulfill your wildest dreams, or do you just want to keep chatting about them with your friends, until one day you wake up as a grumpy, old, frustrated person?
Big achievements require brave and fearless actions. If you want to act bravely, you need to be confident.

Along with lots of useful, practical exercises, this book will provide you with plenty of new information that will help you understand what confidence problems really come down to. And this is the most important and the saddest part, because most people do not truly recognize the root problem, and that's why they get poor results.

Lack of self-confidence and problems with unhealthy self-esteem are usually the reason why smart, competent, and talented people never achieve a satisfying life; a life that should easily be possible for them.

In this book, you will read about:
-How, when, and why society robs us all of natural confidence and healthy self-esteem.
-What kind of social and psychological traps you need to avoid in order to feel much calmer, happier, and more confident.
-What "natural confidence" means and how it becomes natural.
-What "self-confidence" really is and what it definitely isn't (as opposed to what most people think!).
-How your mind hurts you when it really just wants to help you, and how to stop the process.
-What different kinds of fear we feel, where they come from, and how to defeat them.
-How to have a great relationship with yourself.
-How to use stress to boost your inner strength.
-Effective and ineffective ways of building healthy self-esteem.
-Why the relation between self-acceptance and stress is so crucial.
-How to stay confident in professional situations.
-How to protect your self-esteem when life brings you down, and how to deal with criticism and jealousy.
-How to use neuro-linguistic programming, imagination, visualizations, diary entries, and your five senses to re-program your subconscious and get rid of "mental viruses" and detrimental beliefs that actively destroy your natural confidence and healthy self-esteem.
Take the right action and start changing your life for the better today!

DOWNLOAD FOR FREE from Amazon Kindle Store:
https://tinyurl.com/IanConfidenceTraining
Paperback version on Createspace:
http://tinyurl.com/IanConfidencePaperbackV

Mindfulness: The Most Effective Techniques: Connect With Your Inner Self to Reach Your Goals Easily and Peacefully

Mindfulness is not about complicated and otherworldly woo-woo spiritual practices. It doesn't require you to be a part of any religion or a movement.

What mindfulness is about is living a good life (that's quite practical, right?), and this book is all about deepening your awareness, **getting to know yourself**, and developing attitudes and mental habits that will make you not only a successful and effective person in life, but a happy and wise one as well.

If you have ever wondered what the mysterious words "mindfulness" means and why would anyone bother, you have just found your (detailed) answer!

This book will provide you with actionable steps and valuable information, all in plain English, so all of your doubts will be soon gone.

In my experience, **nothing has proven as simple and yet effective and powerful as the daily practice of mindfulness.**

It has helped me become more decisive, disciplined, focused, calm, and just a happier person.

I can come as far as to say that mindfulness has transformed me into a success.

Now, it's your turn.
There's nothing to lose, and so much to win!

The payoff is nothing less than transforming your life into its true potential.

What you will learn from this book:

-What exactly does the word "mindfulness" mean, and why should it become an important word in your dictionary?

-How taking **as little as five minutes a day** to clear your mind might result in steering your life towards great success and becoming a much more fulfilled person? ...and **how the heck can you "clear your mind" exactly?**

-What are the **most interesting, effective, and not well-known mindfulness techniques for success** that I personally use to stay on the track and achieve my goals daily while feeling calm and relaxed?

-**Where to start** and how to slowly get into mindfulness to avoid unnecessary confusion?

-What are the **scientifically proven profits** of a daily mindfulness practice?

-**How to develop the so-called "Nonjudgmental Awareness"** to win with discouragement and negative thoughts, **stick to the practice** and keep becoming a more focused, calm, disciplined, and peaceful person on a daily basis?

-What are **the most common problems** experienced by practitioners of mindfulness and meditation, and how to overcome them?

-How to meditate and **just how easy** can it be?

-What are **the most common mistakes** people keep doing when trying to get into meditation and mindfulness? How to avoid them?

-**Real life tested steps** to apply mindfulness to everyday life to become happier and much more successful person?

-What is the relation between mindfulness and life success? How to use mindfulness to become much more effective in your life and achieve your goals much easier?

-**What to do in life** when just about everything seems to go wrong?

-How to become a **more patient and disciplined person**?

Stop existing and start living.
Start changing your life for the better today.

DOWNLOAD FOR FREE from Amazon Kindle Store:

myBook.to/IanMindfulnessGuide
Paperback version on Createspace:

http://tinyurl.com/IanMindfulnessGuide

Meditation for Beginners: How to Meditate (as an Ordinary Person!) to Relieve Stress and Be Successful

Meditation doesn't have to be about crystals, hypnotic folk music and incense sticks! **Forget about sitting in unnatural and uncomfortable positions while going, "Ommmmm...."** It is not necessarily a club full of yoga masters, Shaolin monks, hippies and new-agers.

It is a super useful and universal practice which can improve your overall brain performance and happiness. When meditating, you take a step back from actively thinking your thoughts, and instead see them for what they are. The reason why meditation is helpful in reducing stress and attaining peace is that it gives your over-active consciousness a break.

Just like your body needs it, your mind does too!

I give you the gift of peace that I was able to attain through present moment awareness.

Direct Buy Link to Amazon Kindle Store:
https://tinyurl.com/IanMeditationGuide
Paperback version on Createspace: **http://tinyurl.com/ianmeditationpaperback**

Zen: Beginner's Guide: Happy, Peaceful and Focused Lifestyle for Everyone

Contrary to popular belief, Zen is not a discipline reserved for monks practicing Kung Fu. Although there is some truth to this idea, Zen is a practice that is applicable, useful and pragmatic for anyone to study regardless of what religion you follow (or don't follow).

Zen is the practice of studying your subconscious and **seeing your true nature.** The purpose of this work is to show you how to apply and utilize the teachings and essence of Zen in everyday life in the Western society. I'm not really an "absolute truth seeker" unworldly type of person—I just believe in practical plans and blueprints that actually help in living a better life. Of course I will tell you about the origin of Zen and the traditional ways of practicing it, but I will also show you my side of things, my personal point of view and translation of many Zen truths into a more "contemporary" and practical language.
It is a "modern Zen lifestyle" type of book.

What You Will Read About:
• Where Did Zen Come from? - A short history and explanation of Zen
• What Does Zen Teach? - The major teachings and precepts of Zen
• Various Zen meditation techniques that are applicable and practical for everyone!
• The Benefits of a Zen Lifestyle
• What Zen Buddhism is NOT?
• How to Slow Down and Start Enjoying Your Life
• How to Accept Everything and Lose Nothing
• Why Being Alone Can Be Beneficial
• Why Pleasure Is NOT Happiness
• Six Ways to Practically Let Go
• How to De-clutter Your Life and Live Simply
• "Mindfulness on Steroids"
• How to Take Care of Your Awareness and Focus
• Where to Start and How to Practice Zen as a Regular Person
• And many other interesting concepts...

I invite you to take this journey into the peaceful world of Zen Buddhism with me today!
Direct Buy Link to Amazon Kindle Store: https://tinyurl.com/IanZenGuide

Paperback version on Createspace: http://tinyurl.com/IanZenPaperbackV

Buddhism: Beginner's Guide: Bring Peace and Happiness to Your Everyday Life

Buddhism is one of the most practical and simple belief systems on this planet, and it has greatly helped me on my way to become a better person in every aspect possible. In this book I will show you what happened and how it was.

No matter if you are totally green when it comes to Buddha's teachings or maybe you have already heard something about them—this book will help you systematize your knowledge and will inspire you to learn more and to take steps to make your life positively better!

I invite you to take this beautiful journey into the graceful and meaningful world of Buddhism with me today!

Direct link to Amazon Kindle Store: https://tinyurl.com/IanBuddhismGuide
Paperback version on Createspace: http://tinyurl.com/ianbuddhismpaperback

About The Author

Author's blog: www.mindfulnessforsuccess.com
Author's Amazon profile: amazon.com/author/iantuhovsky
Instagram profile: https://instagram.com/mindfulnessforsuccess

Hi! I'm Ian...

. . . and I am interested in life. I am in the study of having an awesome and passionate life, which I believe is within the reach of practically everyone. I'm not a mentor or a guru. I'm just a guy who always knew there was more than we are told. I managed to turn my life around from way below my expectations to a really satisfying one, and now I want to share this fascinating journey with you so that you can do it, too.

I was born and raised somewhere in Eastern Europe, where Polar Bears eat people on the streets, we munch on snow instead of ice cream and there's only vodka instead of tap water, but since I make a living out of several different businesses, I move to a new country every couple of months. I also work as an HR consultant for various European companies.

I love self-development, traveling, recording music and providing value by helping others. I passionately read and write about social psychology, sociology, NLP, meditation, mindfulness, eastern philosophy, emotional intelligence, time management, communication skills and all of the topics related to conscious self-development and being the most awesome version of yourself.

Breathe. Relax. Feel that you're alive and smile. And never hesitate to contact me!

Printed in France by Amazon
Brétigny-sur-Orge, FR